13 for Corwin

Barricade Books Inc.
New Jersey

Published by Barricade Books Inc.
1530 Palisade Avenue
Fort Lee, NJ 07024

Distributed by Publishers Group West
4065 Hollis
Emeryville, CA 94608

Printed in the United States of America.

Library of Congress Cataloging-in-Publication Data

13 for Corwin: a paean of praise for Norman Corwin, the #1 writer-producer-director during radio's golden age.
p. cm.
ISBN 0-942637-89-5: $7.95
1. Corwin, Norman Lewis, 1910– 2. Authors, American—20th century—Biography. 3. Radio producers and directors—United States—Biography. 4. Radio plays, American—History and criticism. I. Title: Thirteen for Corwin.
PS3505.0777Z515 1993
814'.52—dc20
[B] 92-38802
CIP

0 9 8 7 6 5 4 3 2 1

Publisher's Proem

Norman Corwin has always been one of my heroes. I grew up with radio. I was nourished by radio. I was educated by radio. Radio made every person a poet—for with radio, the listener had to use imagination or the whole thing didn't work. Radio wasn't the mindless vacuum that became television. It was lively. It was entertaining. It was often challenging.

Every mountain has a summit and at the summit of the radio broadcasting mountain was this fellow named Norman Corwin. No World War II veteran like myself will ever forget Corwin's *On A Note of Triumph*. Ah, but there was so much else of Corwin not as serious. So much that was fun. And so much of Corwin's love of language and thought that was infectious.

Eventually I came to know Norman Corwin and that friendship is warm and rich—for this fellow called Corwin is a most unusual man: kind, generous, warm and brilliant.

When I heard that there was to be a birthday party—a 75th—at the Beverly Hilton hotel, I cashed in my Coca-Cola cans and scraped together the airfare for the journey to the west coast. It was a worthwhile pilgrimage. The party was celebrity-packed. Among the hundreds present, I doubt there was a person who didn't love and admire the man they were celebrating.

One of the birthday gifts was this book—handsomely bound and written with affection and respect. Each guest received one. I happened to reread my copy a few months ago—and I knew that it was selfish not to share it with those not fortunate enough to be in attendance.

—Lyle Stuart

Contents

Introduction

Ray Bradbury

Collected here, what do we find?

Norman Corwin's children.

For if we are not all his children, what are we?

Without knowing what he was up to, for he was busy writing, directing, and producing for radio, Norman Corwin looked around one day and found all these kids on his doorstep.

So here is a proper hierarchy. Not one of brute power, but the magnificent strength that comes with poetry that pulls the soul and changes lives. There isn't a name here that hasn't been so influenced by this kind and talented human being.

If ever a man represented the basic tenet of good Dr. Schweitzer, Norman Corwin is it. Schweitzer said, do something good, someone may imitate it.

Norman, if I can drop into the familiar mode, not only did something good, but better, best, and magnificent.

He called to his many sons, and a gaggle of daughters, across and around the world in 1939. I have told the story before, but it needs a capsuled re-telling.

One Sunday that year, turning on the old parlor radio, I heard someone wind up and toss his voices, and a mob of sounds twenty or thirty times around our planet. The echoes that rushed back, knocked me head over heels into love. Who is this genius, so adept at throwing his voice? I wondered.

Corwin, or course.

I was not alone that afternoon. It was the beginning of the gathering in of the Corwin clan, whose tribe, since those days, has only increased.

What did we teenagers and big-eared fans in their twenties learn from switching off Bob Hope and switching on Norman?

Language and ideas. Ideas and language.

No use having language if you have nothing to say.

No use having ideas if you haven't the words to make the metaphors to express them.

He taught us then not only how to open our mouths but how to insert bright pebbles beneath our tongues so that eventually we migh fire forth a sentence not only worth listening to but thinking about.

I couldn't afford books in those days, so I ran to the library, and as each o Norman Corwin's books of radio plays was published I hauled it home and sat as student reading the master. Because of him I rediscovered Whitman, Wolfe, and, indirectly, Shakespeare and Shaw. In sum he gave me the greatest gift any man can giv another: to dare to speak in great tongues, hoping to find, alon the way, a perhaps dilapidated but great notion.

When it came time for me to write for radio, when I was twenty-six, you could hear Corwin's poetry warping and woofing all the way through my first half hour for the World Security Workshop.

Along the way, of course, I realized I couldn't go on being Norman Corwi forever, and would have to strike out on my own. But his fingerprint tattoos remain all over me, to this day. I would neve have dared my first book of poetry, if he had not started me on the road, the year after I graduated from high school.

This, I am sure, must be the story of every man or woman here collected t cry huzzah. Norman used his power well, not to bruise us but touch us to fly. Because of him, I jumped from a tree and made it to earth without being killed.

Now I will let the others speak for themselves.

Ending with a final, and familiar story.

When I published my first book, *Dark Carnival,* in 1947, I somehow got Norman's phone number and address from a conniving secretary at CBS Radio. I sent Norman my book with a note saying "If you like my book as much as I love you and your work, please let me buy you a drink some afternoon."

A few days later, Norman called and said, "You're not buying me drinks, I'm buying you *dinner!*"

The dinner has lasted forever.

And what a feast!

To the Bard

Studs Terkel

For me, there are two reasons to celebrate May 8, 1945. It was, of course, V-E Day. The war in Europe was over. It was also the day *On a Note of Triumph* was broadcast over CBS. Even now, some 40 years later, I hear the voices. And the words. Oh, those words. They were Norman Corwin's. Of course.

He was the bard of radio's Golden Age. It was no contest. In his giftedness, style and substance were fused. Sound and meaning were equally lyrical. Consider this:

Lord God of test tube and blueprint

Who jointed molecules of dust and shook them till their name was Adam,

Who taught worms and stars how they could live together,

Appear now among the parliaments of conquerors and give instructions to their schemes:

Measure out new liberties so none shall suffer for his father's color or the credo of his choice....

Post proofs that brotherhood is not so wild a dream as those who profit by postponing it pretend:

Sit at the treaty table and convoy the hopes of little peoples through
expected straits,

And press into the final seal a sign that peace will come for long than posterities can see ahead.

That man unto his fellow man shall be a friend forever.

To read it in print is an exhilarant; but to read it aloud or to *hear* it is manifoldly so. Style and substance glued together with the attribute of hope. Hope, a spirit that today, a bewildered today evokes the weary shrug (unfortunately, justified), was *there* when Corwin sang of it. It was this voice that sounded off the Golden Age: a decade, give or take a year: 1938–48.

We are told that things were more simple then; that verities were more clearly defined. You could tell good from evil back in those day Today, oh dear, issues are so much more complex. Oh yeah?

When in early 1939, CBS broadcast Norman Corwin's radio play, *They Fl Through the Air,* it astonished us because it was the first time t bombing of civilians was challenged, in an art form. Sure, ther were demonstrations, here and there; bleeding hearts and bloo ied heads: Stop Fascist Bombing of Ethiopia. There were alway these bothersome ones who would disturb our sleep.

The great many of us heard other voices, powerful and highly respectable ones, celebrating Il Duce's achievements. He did make the train run on time, didn't he? He did deal in no nonsense fashion wit those troublesome labor unions, didn't he? Why, shortly before the explosives were dropped on primitively equipped innocent Mussolini's Air Minister, Italo Balbo, led a glorious flight acros the Atlantic to Chicago. He was greeted by Mayor Kelly and multitudes. We have a thoroughfare named Balbo Street. Thus we still honor a warrior who let Ethiopians have it. Things simpler then? Who is kidding whom?

It took an artist—just as it took Picasso to memorialize an analogous horror, Guernica—to bring this matter to mind and to conscience. This Norman Corwin did. And then some.

Everything he has written and produced (for it was also the moment to be captured and celebrated) has been of one piece. Name it —*Pursuit of Happiness, 13 by Corwin,* his *One World* series, his *Bill of Rights* sesquicentennial program, call out any one—and you will find a soaring sermon (in the bardic sense) on Possibility. And a bull's eye on "those who profit by postponing it."

Thus, his most recent work, *Trivializing America.* "You go right from sinking a cruiser with 300 men dying to a Toyota and a guy leaping in the air with joy that he's bought a Toyota. The lines that formerly separated taste from vulgarity, discretion from rashness, morality from immorality, have become obscured and it all becomes one big matzo ball."

Patently, Corwin's hand is still on the plow, his eye on the prize. His polemic against those who would flatten us out (and who appear to be succeeding) is by its eloquent nature a plea for that which would raise us. It is not a note of triumph he is sounding; it is a note of challenge. Against the odds, perhaps; which is why it is all the more stirring.

Bless Norman Corwin's indignation. And his voice.

From Robert Nathan

We had been sitting in front of our TV set, watching the CBS anniversary celebration; and now it was time for Walter Cronkite's ending words, his summing up, and I settled back for the usual closing remarks. But they didn't come out as I had expected. "That embarkation," he was saying, "is barely started for Andromeda, cruising at the speed of starlight . . ." and he went on, smiling hi gentle, serious smile . . . "The time at the tone, the weather will be, and now for a word . . . the coming of wars and freeways . . ." and I began to sit up and look uneasily around me; was this Cronkite? "No eye has roved like the video eye away and beyon the reach of earth out to the moon and onto it." And as he went on, I found myself more and more uneasy, obscurely disturbed and excited, with a curious lifting of spirit, almost a memory o something young and high-hearted and far away. Until . . . wait moment! I cried, that isn't Cronkite! I know that voice, those singing words, those sweeping rhythms, I know them from somewhere long ago, from someone . . . By God! It's Corwin!

I watch Cronkite, and I hear him: "When at last this reaches you, know th it went out from a small planet with one moon and a billion families." But it is Corwin I hear, and I am suddenly young agai and my heart lifts as it used to in the long-ago dark years, and t old sense of happiness and greatness touches me, and for a moment is with me again.

2 The Spoken Word

CHARLES KURALT

Norman Corwin can do anything with words. Once he wrote a radio play about chemistry. He wrote it all in verse. If he walked into one of the network offices today and said, "I have a play here, in verse, about chemistry," they'd call a guard to assist him to the street. Corwin's play about chemistry starred Groucho Marx, Robert Benchley, Vincent Price, Sylvia Sidney, and Keenan Wynn, among others. It was wonderful. Wonderful words have vanished from the air.

I wonder what Bach thought when he heard other composers play their organ pieces. I wonder what Ty Cobb thought when he watched other players try to hit and run the bases. I wonder what Corwin, who lobbed words through the atmosphere like mortar shells, thinks now when he listens to the radio.

The salesmen are in all the command posts of broadcasting. The poets have been busted to buck private and assigned to peeling potatoes and writing commercials. Words on the air are inert, empty shells that don't explode.

As for journalists, they are enlisted mainly to look sharp in the parades. If they keep their buttons polished and their hair trimmed, they'll do well.

I sit on the edge of the bed in the Holiday Inn at six o'clock in the evening, watching television. Urgent electronic music plays, the lights come up and a young man says to the camera, "Good evening, here is the news." He is earnest and attractive. He wouldn't know a news story if it jumped up and mussed his coiffure.

He is working in Wichita, but he comes from North Bergen, New Jersey, and he is thinking about Denver, the market to which he would like to move next. (These "anchors" speak of places as "markets," having fallen into the jargon of the salesmen who hired them.) What attracts him to Denver is the fact that Denver is bigger than Wichita and the pay is better and the exposure is greater. None of these, if you stop to think about it, is an imperative of journalism. But this young man is a *broadcast* journalist. He can't think, can't write, cares nothing about issues or events, has no sense of history, and does not even know much about the community to which he says, "Good evening, here is the news," while waiting to hear from the station manager in Denver.

He went to college and has a degree in "speech / broadcasting." Nobody ever told him writing has anything to do with it. He'll go far. None of this is his fault. Real journalism is possible on television, but not often tried.

Journalists, real ones, have inside them a little tickle that makes them want to tell stories, to nose around and find out things that are not generally known, and write it all down clearly so people can understand it, and spread the word.

Good stories almost always take a little time to tell. In television as it has come to be practiced, there never is enough time. The salesman who runs the station, knowing nothing about news, has hired a news consultant from far away to advise him. This consultant is a breed of scoundrel. He goes everywhere, giving bad advice.

First, he tells the station manager, you must have ringing bells and flashing graphics to seize the attention of the sap at home who might otherwise be inclined to read a book or play with his children. Then you must keep the show *moving* to dazzle the sucker. Put those reporters out there *live* at the *scene.* Doesn't matter *what* scene. What matters is *live!* What matters is *pace!* Keep it fast and loud: the one-sentence interview, the car wreck on the highway, and bring on the weatherman!

There is a rule at many stations, though you will think I am making this up, that no story is worth more than 90 seconds. These wretched consultants would cut the *Iliad* or *King Lear* to 90 seconds. The station managers who employ them eagerly follow their contemptible advice, and in city after city ("market" after "market") the news is cheapened and the viewer is cheated.

Words have nothing to do with any of this. Nobody thinks about the words.

The young writer who has the old wish to tell stories—the wish that animated the wandering minstrels of the Middle Ages and the bards of old, that makes us remember Dickens and Kipling and Twain—can find no place for himself in radio and television. Too bad. If he is one who feels the little tickle that puts the foreign correspondent on the night plane to Cairo and the city-side reporter on the subway to the Bronx and sends the country weekly editor down to the county treasurer's office for one more look at those records, he will find himself defeated and alone in television news, which has hardly any place left for storytelling.

I don't know how this happened, though I have watched it happen. They had a book of Corwin's plays in the school library in North Carolina. I read it at 13 and knew what I wanted to try to do with my life. At 23, I walked into CBS News and looked around the newsroom with wide eyes. There was Murrow, in shirt-sleeves and galluses. There were Robert Trout and Charles Collingwood and Eric Sevareid. Winston Burdette checked in from Rome and Hottelet from Bonn. They were thinkers, reporters. Writers.

Words counted with them and they knew how to make words count. Sevareid, perhaps the best of them all with words, never felt comfortable with television's lights and lenses and paraphernalia. In one of his grumpier moods he was heard to mutter, "One good word is worth a thousand pictures." Exactly. That's what we forgot.

We still have writers on the premises but the giants are all gone, the ones who made me so proud, once, to be a sapling in that forest of stout old trees. I don't know where the great reporters will come from to teach their standards to another generation, but I'm pretty sure they won't come from that station in Wichita.

Maybe I am wrong. Maybe weariness and memory have made me unreasonably cynical about broadcasting's present and future. Maybe this darkness is the sort that comes before the dawn, and the few mature and responsible newsrooms will be templates for newsrooms of the future. Maybe the best news directors will become managers of their stations. Maybe good judgments will replace greed in the front offices. Maybe a comet will come from heaven and burn all the news consultants to ashes.

Twenty-five years ago, Ed Murrow, acknowledging the miraculous technology that was becoming available, warned that a television set is just a box with wires. What appears on the screen depends upon the imagination and creativity of human beings. Since then, the shining promise of the box with wires has so seldom been fulfilled that we've forgotten how bright it was. We know how television is done now, and that's the way we go on doing it. The imaginative and creative men and women, the writers, have mostly drifted away to seek their fortunes elsewhere.

Writing words to be spoken on the air is an odd occupation to begin with, of course. It is no field for anybody with intimations of immortality. One's best work speeds away, literally at the speed of light, never to be heard again. You get used to it. You know you're working for the evening news, not for the ages. Luckily, some of Norman Corwin's words were collected from the ether and put in books. The other night, unable to sleep, I put on my bathrobe and looked through the bookshelves until I found the one I was looking for.

I had been listening to a Cabinet member declaring, on one of the late-night talk shows, that the country must arm itself with a new generation of long-range missiles in order to "retain our nuclear credibility." Nobody else on the program put up much of an argument. "Credibility" seemed such a grotesque word for what the man meant that I wanted to read some better words on the subject.

Corwin wrote them a few weeks after the Hiroshima bomb went off. They were in the book I first came across in the school library:

> ...the atom can be far more sullen than has yet been shown.
>
> Attack it with another thrust of algebraic symbols and the cutting edge of an equation, and there will be the grand reaction:
>
> The first news of it will arrive in your precinct as a shuddering in the sky:
>
> A glow, far off, brightening: heat beating outward in concentric waves: the atmosphere a band of fire: the seas themselves, the wet seas, tinder:

The hills that looked on Christ will heave and crackle, and quarries vaporize as eagerly as the dust of Pharaohs:

The earth, the tamed and tonsured earth, with all its gardens and substances, its places, breeds, and patterns, its letters and its airs, will plummet out of grace; will fail its orbit,

And soon enough will be a blistered ash, its moon trailing lonely and ungoverned, like a dog after its master's corpse.

Do not smile, do not smile as though knowing better.

It could happen.

The model is any suicide.

The model is Sampson, destroying the temple and himself....

I wanted to say the words out loud, as an answer to the Cabinet member. Cabinet members, like the rest of us, no longer hear such words now that the writers have lost their air time.

3

Letter to The World

NORMAN LEAR

It has been said that literature is the result of a solitary individual sitting down alone in a room at a particular point in history to paint some word-images for the rest of humanity; "my letter to the world" is how Emily Dickinson described her poetry. What really intrigues me, now that the broadcast media have replaced literature as the most accessible popular art, is what kind of "letters to the world" are being written today for commercial broadcasting. Are they art? Are they boilerplate? Do they inspire and inform? Or do they anesthetize? Are they worth our attention?

These questions are timely because the broadcast media as currently operated have trouble finding room for individual creativity and experimentation. In television, the video "letters to the world" are sponsored by corporate networks whose committees of executives and market researchers must approve new shows and concepts. Naturally, the end result reflects their biases. Yet the most meaningful, entertaining broadcasting, I have learned, has a singularity of voice. The vision of one person, projecting a moral tone or provocative idea with grace and style, is always more compelling than the handiwork of a committee. Furthermore, a network committee usually keeps a sharp eye on maximizing return on investment; an individual writer or producer is more oriented to his or her craft. A television network, for example, usually believes that speeding cars, braless girls on motorcycles, and fistfights will help boost a show's ratings. A scriptwriter, on the other hand, generally has more interest in developing characters, building dramatic tension, and exploring complexity in human relationships. When it is time to rewrite a script, the network programming department, armed with research indicating that a little violence did well last season, will confront the writer and ask: "Where's the action? You've got a seven-page scene here with two people talking!" In the wink of an eye, the scene is moved from a living room to a car. The driver is so intent on his discussion that he veers off the road and careens down an embankment, injured bodies spill out, and the car explodes in flames. That's action.

Such is the inevitable conflict in commercial broadcasting today. The real challenge facing the broadcast media, I believe, is for it to live up to its immense creative possibilities: to make a system of "mass communication with commercial goals to speak meaningfully to *individuals.*

One of the earliest broadcasters to master this challenge and celebrate it through his work was Norman Corwin. Hailed by *The New Yorker* in 1947 as "America's most prominent radio play-wright," Corwin introduced a new personal, dramatic dimension to the medium of radio. In the process, he enriched his listeners' lives, American culture, and the evolving art of broadcasting.

Corwin's passion was, and is, to expand the universe of sounds heard and feelings felt by radio listeners. (Happily for all of us, he has also chosen to share his keen observations on our culture in essays and books, most recently and notably in the widely acclaimed *Trivializing America.)* In one of his first breakthroughs, Corwin convinced the program director of New York City's WQXR to allow him to recite verse over the air and discuss it, every Wednesday night. After one such performance, CBS took note of Corwin and asked him to put together a similar program to popularize great literature. But that experiment was cut short by a sudden reassignment to direct *Americans at Work* and *Living History,* two new radio shows that gave Corwin valuable production experience.

Another Corwin innovation was *The Plot to Overthrow Christmas,* a rhymed fantasy which aired on Christmas Day 1938. This was followed in 1939 with the *Words Without Music* series, which melded verse, drama, narrative, and sound effects into powerful new combinations. Other rich dramas would follow: *They Fly Through the Air with the Greatest of Ease, We Hold These Truths, On a Note of Triumph,* and dozens of others.

The *experience* of listening to a Corwin radio drama cannot be faithfully translated to text. The sounds and pace and elements of surprise and recognition create a signature Corwin style. A critic for the *Saturday Review,* apparently stumped at how to describe a Corwin drama to his readers, confessed, "It is hard to describe the power of his images, the variety of his rhythms, the driving conciseness of his phrases, and his happy mixture of the colloquial and the eloquent." But, concluded the critic, "Mr. Corwin's mind, his style and his conscience all have muscles."

Especially in matters of timely national import—such as World War II—Corwin illuminated the moral landscape with his broadcasts, drawing upon his skills as a reporter, writer, poet, scriptwriter, director, and producer. CBS, to its lasting credit, gave Corwin the latitude to experiment and follow his impulses.

All of Norman Corwin's innovations in radio strike me as memorable because they represent a spirit in broadcasting that is now endangered. Corwin exemplified the virtues of honing a personal vision, taking risks with new techniques, and trying to find something fresh in a familiar yet malleable medium, radio. What made Corwin's radio career so remarkable was not just his personal artistic sensibilities but his triumph over an industry that puts a premium on the predictable.

By coincidence, a single page of *Time* magazine in 1946 which featured an article about Corwin illustrates the creative constraints of radio at the time. One story on the page reported that Corwin had just won two prestigious broadcasting awards within one week, making him "radio's 35-year-old wonder boy." The other story lamented the cancellation of a bright new radio show because of its low ratings. It is worth excerpting this latter item because it could have been written yesterday:

> One of radio's newest and freshest programs *Request Performance,* was sacked last week by Campbell's Soup, effective April 21. Reason: the show's Hooper and Crossley ratings were not high enough.
>
> *The New York Times'* Radio Editor Jack Gould wrote: "Ratings are perhaps the biggest cross that radio has to bear and now would be a fine time to heave them out.... The rating...has been exaggerated to such an extreme that broadcasting has

come to operate on a meretricious set of values. Whether a program has an intrinsic merit of its own is no longer the prime question."

The *Times'* radio critic went on to charge the rating system with fulfilling "the sinister function of being the absolute critical standard for radio programming. It is as though a Rembrandt, a Beethoven symphony, a burlesque comic, a Tin Pan Alley ballad, a Keats sonnet and a pulp-magazine serial all were to be weighed on the same scales. That would seem too much even for radio."

Perhaps. But nearly 40 years later, simplistic ratings have *not* proven "too much" for radio nor its sister industry, television. The most radically different shows are willy-nilly subjected to the monocular judgment of "objective" ratings. And those programs that cannot garner a quick and powerful response from America's jaded TV viewers are axed. "How many viewers?" is the preeminent concern, not "how good is the show?" And lost in the dung heap of early cancellations are those innovative efforts that might have appealed to the *best* instincts of American viewers had they been allowed the time to become acquired tastes.

This syndrome bedeviled radio in Norman Corwin's time; it has since intensified greatly and come to exercise sweeping influence in determining what "letters to the world" are broadcast on radio and television. And the networks' overreliance on contrived rating systems not only impoverishes us culturally, it is bad business. Allow me to explain.

The name of the game for the television networks, when they are deciding what ideas are worthy of air time, is: "How do I win Tuesday night at 8 o'clock?" They do not ask, for example, "How do I program responsibly in the long-range interest of the viewer?" They do not ask themselves how the sex, harm, and violence they program may be affecting our children. They do not ask, "How do I innovate, how do I re-invent the wheel so as to keep network television consistently changing and maturing in the long-range interest of the shareholder?" Their concern is simply: "How do I win Tuesday night at 8 o'clock."

I submit that when the only criterion for selecting a show is how it may rate against the competition in the short term, it is not good for network *business* in the long term. Despite the writing on the wall—namely, the onslaught of new communications technologies that could partially supplant TV—we now see CBS, the former patron of Norman Corwin, sitting complacently, repeating itself endlessly. And we observe the other two networks scrambling, *not* to innovate, but to imitate. Innovation is shunned because it requires risk-taking, and risk-taking is antithetical to winning in the short term. And so, with painful predictability, the networks putter with the same tired formats, adding more sex here and more violence there— more mindlessness—in an effort to grab the cynical viewers' attention quickly. If the heads of the three networks were standing in a circle with razors to each other's throats, they could not be committing suicide more deliberately.

It is one of the great ironies of the twentieth century that one of its most awesome inventions, television, is surrendering its potential to educate, nurture, and inspire as it entertains and informs. Broadcasts of the sort pioneered by Norman Corwin stand in towering contrast to the flotsam and jetsam of most of today's broadcast fare. This nation's addiction to the inconsequential and gratuitous was examined at some length by Norman Corwin in his recent aforementioned book, *Trivializing America,* in which he decried the "forces in our culture and society that tend to reduce us, to fragment our concentration, erode our standards, fritter away our native genius, and make our political procedures a kind of National Trifle Association...."

Trivialization on television is symptomatic of a much more pervasive disease in our society. To my mind, the single most destructive societal disease of our time is American leadership's fixation with what has come to be known as the short-term "bottom line." Whether it is in industry, government, or academe, leadership everywhere seems all too ready to sell the future short for a moment of success. It is a pandemic affliction in our society.

Consider how the Big Three automakers for years refused to innovate and build small, fuel-efficient automobiles. They refused to sacrifice a quarterly profit statement in order to invest more in the future, to meet the threat of imports from abroad. Or consider the steel companies who refused to modernize their facilities and reinvest in themselves. Or how the labor unions in *both* industries fought only for added wages and benefits instead of fighting to modernize and upgrade their industries and thereby protect their members' jobs in the long term. It's all part of a national addiction to quick fixes, a radically narrow sense of self-interest, and a pathological aversion to long-term commitments and risks.

What makes this disease of the spirit so difficult to combat is that there are really no single villains. It is a matter of climate. The average network programming executive, for example, is trapped. Imagine yourself in this job: You wake up in the morning and read in *The New York Times* that your network did not have one show in the Top Ten. Your palms sweat. On your way into the office, you pick up *The Wall Street Journal* which now prints an analysis of projected earnings based on ratings. Your network's projected earnings are down. You walk into the office and a warm photocopy of last night's overnight ratings is on your desk. You didn't win a single time slot.

Now your first appointment of the day is with tomorrow's Norman Corwin, or Rod Serling, or Paddy Chayefsky who has a fresh, innovative idea. I submit that you are in no condition to hear a new idea. What you must have, and quickly, is a new version of something that is working on one of the other networks. You are a victim; trapped.

Television must, of course, pay attention to business and prosper economically. But it must never overlook the *human* essence, that spirit that defies the marketplace and its economic calculus of motives. Television must realize that creativity—entrepreneurial talent—ultimately does not respond to the demands of the market alone. It responds to other stimuli, such as human nurturance. If confined to a regimented environment such as that created by Sweeps Weeks and other rating obsessions, creativity and entrepreneurialism wilt. But if allowed to explore and take risks, and sometimes fail, creativity, the entrepreneurial instinct, and the search for excellence will flourish. And where it flourishes, success and return on investment will follow.

In radio and television, it is absurd to think that numerical ratings can actually predict the "success" or value of unique human utterances—jokes, dramas, documentaries, comedies, entertainment shows, and the rich palette of self-expression. These require cultivation and nurturance to flourish. Otherwise, only coarse, common types of programming will survive. If, for example, WQXR's Elliott Sanger had not taken a chance on Norman Corwin's poetry broadcasts because they were too unusual or risky, imagine the loss to radio—both financially and artistically. Similarly, if CBS, in the person of Robert Wood, had not taken a leap of faith in a new situation comedy concept called *All in the Family,* the network would effectively have squelched whatever innovation we were fortunate enough to bring to television comedy. And if the network had not given us a somewhat long-term commitment to work out the bugs and try to help our fledgling product catch hold in the marketplace, we would have been dead in the water. As would *M*A*S*H, The Dick Van Dyke Show,* and *The Mary Tyler Moore Show.* These shows succeeded because some executive trusted their guts more than the "scientifically gathered" numbers that purport to judge a program's worth. And they gave the new experiments a chance to succeed in the market over time.

It took *All in the Family* 16 weeks, despite all the controversy surrounding it, to crawl out of the cellar and make a dent in the ratings. In 1983, *a.k.a. Pablo,* the first series to feature a Mexican-American family, was cancelled after only six episodes had aired. It was a show that was not destined to catch on quickly, a show that had to be an acquired taste, but ABC did not feel it could afford to invest in a fresh product and, perhaps, a new audience.

Just how severely we impoverish ourselves by clinging to the false certainties of "hard" ratings such as the Nielsens is not really appreciated. Measuring success through numbers and abstractions has become a highly respected practice in our time, that is true. Consider the indices we live by: SAT scores, the Dow-Jones average, political opinion polls, zip code marketing evaluations, the Gross National Product, the Consumer Price Index. Important as these numbers are, does it really enrich us to orient our behavior so slavishly to these "objective" scales?

American business, for one, is starting to realize that new tools are needed to gauge success in business, and to set broader goals in the first place. In their iconoclastic book on business management, *In Search of Excellence,* Thomas J. Peters and Robert H. Waterman, Jr., point out, for example, that conventional measures of productivity don't "really elaborate on the value of a turned-on Maytag or Caterpillar work force, churning out quality products—or a Frito-Lay salesperson going that extra mile for the ordinary customer." Yet these facts are ultimately as important to a company's success as the criteria used by Standard & Poor.

It is only when a surprise hits us in the face—an Apple computer company, a TV show like *M*A*S*H,* a broadcaster like Norman Corwin —that it becomes clear how suffocating the conventional wisdom has become and how liberating experimentation can be. It is only by loosening our grip on our security blankets of Nielsen ratings that we can free ourselves from obsessional short-term orientations and make better provisions for the future.

Norman Corwin had this sort of ambition for his radio reporting and dramas. When a reporter asked him what he hoped his work would accomplish, he replied, "I hope you'll excuse the pretentious comparison, but I think of the *(One World Flight)* radio series like Pathfinder planes which precede a raid and light a target. My series may not score a hit, but it may light up an area that has not hitherto been explored.... Anyway, it's all there for history, if history is interested.

History is indeed interested. But what of the present? Will the chieftains of the broadcast industry have the courage to allow distinctive, original voices to be heard? And will they afford the time to allow those voices to build an audience? Or will they continue to rely on stale formulas and puffery to keep their industry healthy? As Norman Corwin's distinguished career has shown, excellence, when nurtured, yields a bounty for all of us.

4 The Life of the Mind

NORMAN COUSINS

Norman Corwin, whatever his main areas of public identification, is essentially an educator. He has been engaged in repairing the basic default in education represented by the erroneous and corrosive notion that the central aim of education is to get the highest pay in a good job. The paradox, of course, is that the people who do well at their jobs are those who are able to supercede vocational training. The reason is that they are able to make judgments that proceed out of a highly developed sense of values, a sense of history, a sense of what makes human relationships work, and a sense of timing—all of which are what is meant by a genuine education. It helps to have a sense of theater, as Norman Corwin does, which fits in beautifully with the life of the mind.

Thomas Jefferson was prouder of having been the founder of the University of Virginia than of having been President of the United States. He knew that the educated and developed mind was the best assurance that a political system could be made to work—a system based on the informed consent of the governed. In recent years, however, the Jefferson emphasis on the liberal arts has fallen on hard times. Our universities are under pressure to become job-training centers and employment agencies. The pressure comes mainly from those who want to reduce taxes by cutting back on anything in education that is not connected to skills, or from parents and students who tend to scorn courses of study that do not teach people how to become attractive to employers in a tightening job market. Education is being measured more by the size of the benefits the individual can extract from society than by the extent to which the individual can, in John Dewey's phrase, come into possession of his or her powers.

The irony of the emphasis being placed on careers is that few things are more useful in life than to be able to deal with abstractions or complexities, or to feel comfortable with subtleties of thought or language, or to think sequentially. The doctor who knows only disease is at a disadvantage alongside the doctor who knows at least as much about people as he does about pathological organisms. The lawyer who argues in court from a narrow legal base is no match for the lawyer who can connect legal precedents to historical experience and who employs wide-ranging intellectual resources. The business executive whose competence in general management is bolstered by an artistic ability to deal with people knows how to get the most out of the marketplace. For the technologist, the engineering of consent can be just as important as the engineering of moving parts.

In all these respects, the liberal arts are basic building blocks. Just in terms of career preparation, therefore, a student is only hurting himself by cutting around the humanities. Even if it could be demonstrated that the humanities contribute nothing directly to a job, they would still be an essential part of the educational equipment of any person who wants to come to terms with life. The humanities would be expendable only if human beings didn't have to make decisions that affect their lives and the lives of others; if the human past never existed or had nothing to tell us about the present; if thought processes were irrelevant to the achievement of purpose; if creativity was beyond the human mind and had nothing to do with the joy of living; if human relationships were random aspects of life; if human beings never had to cope with panic or pain, or if they never had to anticipate the connection between cause and effect; if all the mysteries of mind and nature were fully plumbed; and if no special demands arose from the accident of being born a human being instead of a hen or a hog.

The United States Constitution has been described as the most remarkable and enduring political document ever devised by the human mind. The Constitution is not a sheaf of political instructions and strictures but a harvesting of intellectual and cultural riches going back to antiquity. The discussion and debates that went into the making of that document were not confined to operational problems but drew heavily upon the experience and wisdom of the ages. The delegates to the Constitutional Convention were able to undergird their arguments with allusions to the ideas of philosophers, essayists, and dramatists. Names such as Thucydides, Aristotle, Herodotus, Plutarch, or Seneca were commonly cited to support their positions. They alluded to fictional characters from Aristophanes, Marlowe, or Shakespeare to lend color to the exploration of ideas. The analytical essays by Hamilton, Madison, and Jay that appeared in the *The Federalist Papers* were an excursion into the remote corners of history.

Conversation and letters today, like education, have become enfeebled by emphasis on the functional and the purely contemporary. The result is a mechanization not just of the way we live, but of the way we think, and of the human spirit itself.

Men such as Jefferson, Adams, Franklin, and Rush regarded literate conversation as among life's most gratifying exercises. They could summon pertinent quotations from Suetonius or Machiavelli or Montaigne to illustrate a principle. If they referred to Bacon's opinion of Aristotle, they didn't have to cite particulars; they assumed such details were common knowledge. Their allusions were not the product of intellectual ostentation or ornamentation but the natural condiments of discourse, bringing out the full flavor of the cultivated intelligence.

The same was true of correspondence. People regarded letters as an art form and a highly satisfying way of engaging in civilized exchange. The correspondence of Jefferson and Adams and Priestly was not so much a display of personal matters as a review of the human condition. It was not unusual for the writers to range across the entire arena of human thought as a way of sharing perceptions. Allusion was common currency.

In visiting university campuses today, one has the impression that nothing is easier than to get into discussions about job markets or comparative salaries. And nothing is more difficult to discuss than the purposes of education or human potentiality. The result is that we are turning out young men and women who a superbly trained but poorly educated. They are a how-to gene ation, less concerned with the nature of things than with the working of things. They are beautifully skilled but intellectual underdeveloped. They have been separated from tradition and from the creative splendor accumulated over the years by gifte minds. They live without allusion.

The area in which a poor education shows up first is in self-expression, oral or written. It makes little difference how many university courses or degrees a person may own, if he cannot use words to move an idea from one point to another, his education is incomplete. The business of assembling the right words, puttir them down in proper sequence, enabling each one to pull its weight in the conveyance of meaning—these are the essentials. A school is where these essentials would feel at home.

The first purpose of education is to enable a person to speak up and be understood. Incoherence is no virtue. Feeble language is the surest reflection of a feeble mentality. Even as an affectation rather than a basic condition, stereotyped inarticulateness tenc to slow down and cheapen the entire process of communicatior

Not everyone is lucky enough to be wealthy. But no one need be impoverished in language, nor need anyone be deprived of the distinction that comes from using words with strength and grace. The English language may not be as suitable as the German for scientific purposes, especially in medicine; and it may not have the suppleness and music of French; but in range, depth, and precision it is unsurpassed by any other Western language.

Education—the good education that Norman Corwin seems to me to symbolize—can help us to move out beyond the narrow and calcifying confines of the ego so that we can identify ourselves sympathetically—no, that word is not strong enough—identify ourselves *compassionately* with the mainstream of humanity.

The highest expression of civilization is not its art but the supreme tende ness that people are strong enough to feel and show toward or another. Art proceeds out of an exquisite awareness of life. Th creative spirit and the compassionate spirit are not things apart but kindred manifestations of response to life. If our civilization is breaking down, as it appears to be, it is not because we lack the brainpower to meet its demands, but because our feelings are being dulled.

What our society needs is a massive and pervasive experience in resensitization. The first aim of education should not be to prepare young people for careers but to enable them to develop respect for life. Related lessons would be concerned with the reality of human sensitivity and the need to make it ever finer and more responsive; the naturalness of loving and the circumstances that enhance it or enfeeble it; the right to privacy as an essential condition of life; and the need to avoid the callousness that leads to brutalization. Finally, there is the need to endow government with the kind of sensitivity that makes life and all its wondrous possibilities government's most insistent concern.

The conditions of life are inseparable from the conditions of art. The truly creative writer or artist never has to choose between the ivory tower and the arena. He moves freely from one to the other according to his needs and his concerns. The creative process depends least of all upon accident. It requires that the mind be properly worked and tended, that it be given the blessing of silence and the gift of sequence.

An artist, like a philosopher, may draw energy from what he does not know; the deeper the pursuit of the mysteries, the broader and more nourishing it becomes. And, like the scientist, the artist may do things without any clear idea of where he is going. But, as in both philosophy and science, what the artist doesn't know is no warrant for the celebration of ignorance, or for the annihilation of all tradition and the cumulative refinement of technique.

Anyone who wants to pursue the great mysteries must be prepared to struggle with imponderables and take refuge in the imagination. "Let others wrangle, I will wonder," said Saint Augustine.

The ability of words to throw a loop around human personality and to penetrate the inner space of character is exceeded by nothing that can be given visual form. Over the years, in numberless characterizations, attempts have been made to pictorialize Oscar Wilde's Dorian Gray, a depraved, debased, wanton, morally stagnant excuse for a man. Still, the visualization always falls short of the image created by the mind itself out of Wilde's words.

"Creative writing," said John Mason Brown, "is the sweetest agony know to man." He is right. It is the one fatigue that produces inspiration, the exhaustion that exhilarates. Double-teaming the faculties of imagination and reasoning and keeping them coordinated and balanced is a tiring process, but there is something to show for your efforts. Socrates liked to refer to himself as a literary midwife—someone who helped to bring ideas to birth out of laboring minds. As a master of cerebral obstetrics, Socrates also knew and respected the conditions necessary for the conception of ideas.

We have become the most powerful nation in the world, but we exercise less moral influence than at almost any time in our history. W possess unlimited destructive force, but we have not equated that power with a design for peace that people everywhere can identify as the underlying principle of our foreign policy. We are long on force but short on ideas.

We are taking history lightly, trying to ad-lib our way out of challenges that call for deep understanding and moral response. We are chasing after events with a mop rather than trying to build durable instruments of law among nations. We are uncomfortable with terms like "human destiny." If the test before the human species today is whether we are smart enough to survi we are giving little evidence of putting that intelligence to wor

In an early script called *The Charter in the Saucer* which Norman Corwi wrote for United Nations Radio, a flying saucer lands off the coast of Ireland manned by one lone space voyager. He has co from a planet surfeited with problems—famine, wars, depressions, sickness, insecurity, and worst of all, stupidity. By hove ing over planet earth and intercepting radio waves, he has bee hoping to find ideas that would improve life on his planet. He especially impressed by what he calls the "noble sediments" o the Charter of the United Nations, and asks: "Have you been able to combine your efforts to accomplish these aims?"

The challenge Norman Corwin put to us nearly 40 years ago is unmet. Even more serious perhaps is that this failure has occurred in the context of a nuclear age.

But there are hopeful and rising new forces which have their origins not in the actions or plans of government but in the changes coming about within people themselves. The changes have come about so gradually and so unceremoniously that they are not yet a clearly recognizable factor in the survival equation. What is happening is that human consciousness is undergoing a profound expansion. People are less inclined to regard themselves as creatures of circumstance and drift. There is a new sense that the world and everything in it belongs to the people who inhabit it; that wars and famines and homelessness and squalor and disease and filthy air and contaminated water are not inevitable features of the human condition; that people do not have to limp along after history; and that humans were put on earth to overcome their ordeals and not to succumb to them.

The new consciousness is not producing detailed and systematic blueprints for restructuring society or for concocting new turbines and new fuels, nor is it likely in the future to take tangible and quantifiable turns. What it is doing is enabling people to accept responsibility for themselves and for one another. They have a pervasive awareness of their interconnection in a fragile estate. The emergence of the world into a single geographic unit is regarded as an opportunity, not to create an ultimate battlefield, but to develop an interdependent and functional world civilization. People are unwilling to accept governments as the sole custodians of human destiny. They recognize the need for new institutions that accept human life and not machines or armies as the highest value. They do not exempt countries from moral standards that must exist in the relationship among individuals. And when they stand up to be counted, it is as members of the human race, rather than this or that tribe or nation.

Computerized predictions of doom for the human future are wrong. They do not allow for minds like Jefferson or Einstein, minds not paralyzed by the size of problems, minds that are challenged by problems. The important thing is that we have a society in which problems can be openly identified and met.

The American experience has come a long way toward justifying the hopes of the young men in Philadelphia, almost 200 years ago. They felt that the *way* in which the country went about solving its problems was critically important, and that the design of government was inseparable from its formation. A philosophy of government had to be articulated in order to be appraised by the people in an understanding of that philosophy.

Albert Schweitzer—doctor, philosopher, musician, scholar, educator—said he often felt out of step with his time. Yet, from his jungle hospital in equatorial Africa, he maintained a remarkable objectivity and depth of perception of the human scene. He sternly rejected those who would open the sluices to let a flood of skepticism pour itself over the land. "With its depreciation of thinking, our generation has lost its feel for sincerity and with it that for truth as well. It can therefore be helped only by its being brought once more on to the road of thinking. Because I have this certainty, I oppose the spirit of the age and take upon myself with confidence the responsibility to taking my part in the rekindling of the fire of thought." His message to a group of teachers is as profoundly anachronistic as it is welcome: "Start early to instill in your students awareness that they are on this earth to help and serve—that is as important to pass on to them as knowledge."

5

Defendant on Camera

ERIK BARNOUW

I got to know Camilo ("Bud") Leyra well, and we were always on good terms. But it was never easy to put out of mind that he had been found guilty by three different juries of murdering his father and mother, and had spent five years in the death house at Sing Sing awaiting his turn in the electric chair. The fact that Leyra had then gone free—though he was never acquitted of the charges—was a remarkable bit of judicial history. And that, of course, was why I was in touch with him and why we were working together. My assignment was a series of television documentaries on constitutional law, and he had volunteered to assist on a film I was planning on "the Leyra case." He had even expressed willingness to portray himself in reenacted sequences. So there we were, calmly discussing production details.

Meanwhile New York State, which had three times obtained convictions of him and three times run into judicial reversals, seemed unlikely to try him again, but it had a right to. Under these circumstances it was not easy, as we worked on camera angles, locations, dialogue sequences, to sort out one's feelings about Bud Leyra, or about the bizarre situation in which we found ourselves. What did it tell us about television, and how it had perhaps altered the contexts in which we live?

Bud Leyra had at one time been a professional musician, and said he had played in Paul Whiteman's orchestra. But during the Depression he had fallen on difficult times and become a bartender, working for a while at the Stork Club. In 1950, when the Leyra case burst on public attention via *Daily News* headlines and photos, he was working as a bartender in Greenwich Village. He was estranged from his wife, who lived in New Jersey, while he shared an apartment in lower Manhattan with a girl who had a job in a pencil factory. Bud's bartending was mainly an evening activity; in the daytime he was associated with his father in a small business of making and selling typewriter ribbons, which was operated from a loft at the edge of the financial district. Th business was in trouble and was the subject of frequent arguments with his father. According to the prosecution version of the Leyra case, a violent quarrel and his mother's efforts to halt it had led to the murders. When the murdered bodies were in due time found, sprawled in blood in the old couple's Brooklyn apartment, three used teacups were noted on the breakfast tabl suggesting there had been a trusted morning visitor. A few days later, after prolonged grilling, Bud was charged with the murders and brought to trial. Substantial supporting evidence was presented, enough to convince the jury—and later two other juries—of his guilt. He consequently spent the years 1950–55 behind bars. During that time he saw a number of fellow prisoners pass by his cell on their way to the electric chair. He said he and Julius Rosenberg had occupied adjoining cells the night before the Rosenberg execution.

Our documentary series was titled *Decision: The Constitution in Action.* I had been commissioned in 1956 by National Educational Telev sion, a program service set up by a Ford Foundation grant to strengthen the fledgling educational television system. The seri was produced for NET by the Center for Mass Communicatio of Columbia University Press, which began work on the series i 1957. In each of the half-hour films we retraced a recent U.S. Supreme Court case involving a constitutional question—votin rights, censorship, labor standards, military power, and other issues. We had persuaded diverse litigants, lawyers, judges, and others to participate in reenacted sequences, many of them staged in the original locations. One reason for adopting this reenactment technique was that our budget, $17,200 per half-hour film, virtually ruled out the renting of studios or the hirin of actors. The reenacted sequences, supplemented by any relevant newsreel footage that might be available, were in each cas threaded by a running commentary.

By 1959 we had completed six such films. At this juncture our consultant Herbert Wechsler, professor of constitutional law at Columbia University, pointed out one crucial issue of the time that had not been touched and that should probably not be ignored. This was *fair procedure.* In various recent cases criminal convictions had been set aside because of unfair or illegal procedures used to obtain a conviction. In these cases the justices had felt that concern for the integrity of the legal system outweighed questions of guilt or innocence. The most striking case of this sort, thought Wechsler, was probably the recent Leyra case. He suggested I investigate it. So, after studying the record, I visited Leyra's lawyer Frederick Scholem, whose offices were in midtown Manhattan.

Scholem had entered the case as public defender, appointed because Leyra could not afford counsel. Public funds were available only for the original trial, not for appeals. But Scholem told me he had become so enraged by the handling of the case by the Brooklyn police, the prosecution, and even the trial judge, that he became determined to appeal. At one point the judge, according to Scholem, had told him in chambers: "Fred, you'd better plead him guilty. They've found the bloodstained clothing, you know." No bloodstained clothing was ever presented in evidence. This typified the mendacity that Scholem felt had characterized the proceedings. In the end he decided to finance the appeals himself. Their remarkable outcome thus represented Scholem's niche in legal history, and he was eager to take part in the film, including any reenactments.

We then discussed Leyra. The Leyra film seemed to me to present very special problems, of a sort not involved in our other cases. The discovery of the bodies had come a day or so after the event. When the father had failed to appear at the office, and efforts to reach the old couple by phone had failed, Bud Leyra had himself organized an expedition to Brooklyn, in which others had joined him. The apartment had been opened, and the grisly scene revealed. Leyra's behavior throughout these actions was the subject of detailed testimony by several witnesses, and seemed an essential element in the case. In fact, the finding of the bodies had become a key episode in the script I had drafted. To expect Leyra to participate in a reenactment of this kind seemed to me too bizarre for consideration. Even to ask him would seem—I thought at this time—in bad taste. I therefore suggested that we should deviate from our usual procedure an look for a substitute—a look-alike, if possible. There was news reel footage of Leyra's final release from Sing Sing, accompanie by Scholem and associate counsel Osmond K. Fraenkel; this, along with the front-page photos from the *Daily News,* would be usable if a look-alike could be found for the dramatized scenes.

Scholem was entirely amenable. Whatever we decided would be all right with him. He felt he should meanwhile let Leyra know of our plans. I gathered that Leyra had become a bartender in Las Vegas, and was prospering. He had even remarried since going free.

I arranged to meet Scholem again the next week, to discuss a shooting schedule and our casting problem. I would bring Stefan Sharff, who served as producer-director-cameraman-editor for the series, while I did the writing and supervised. We had worked i this way on all the previous films.

When we arrived for our meeting the following week, Scholem had a surprise announcement for us. The moment he had told Leyra what we were doing, Leyra had decided to obtain a leave of absence and head East. He had said he wanted to help. In fact, he was en route. Scholem, looking at his watch, said Leyra mus already have landed. Ten minutes later Bud Leyra walked in th door, and Scholem introduced us. Leyra, a stocky figure neatly dressed in a dark suit, had a quietly cheerful manner. A whiff o perfume preceded him into the room. We stood around awkwardly.

According to my recollection, the conversation then proceeded along thes lines. I said, "Mr. Leyra, I guess you've heard—we're going to make a film about the Leyra case."

"Yes—great. Whatever I can do to help—"

"We're going to dramatize various scenes. You mean you—well, would yo consider playing yourself?"

"Whatever I can do to help."

"Perhaps you should first read the script, before we discuss that. Why don you take this with you? We can meet again tomorrow, if that's convenient, and we'll talk it over."

"Whatever you say. Anything I can do to help."

All this went in a quiet, businesslike manner, but I was uneasy. In writing the script, I had been determined that audiences must understand why three juries had found Leyra guilty, as well as why three appellate courts had voided the convictions. The most damaging evidence against Leyra, as well as against the prosecution, was included in my draft. How would Leyra react to this aspect of the script? Would he be indignant? If so, what form would his anger take?

When we met again the following day, he was as calm as before. He pointed out a small technical error in the script, easily corrected—one which Scholem should have found and hadn't. I began to learn that Leyra knew his case as well as his lawyer did. Leyra explained: he had had five years to study it. He also said he was ready to take part. Both he and Scholem signed our sweeping release forms. They had no objection to the choice of sequences.

I was still uneasy. Conflicting impulses are inherent in any autobiographical project. With the chance to reveal comes a chance to amend —to make things a bit better than they were. In choosing to have people portray themselves we knew we were giving them a degree of control over the portrayals. We gained some authenticity, but with risks. We had accepted the risks because the key scenes in each of our films were based on a legal record. The words were from recorded testimony, or from episodes that were the subject of such testimony. We would not allow deviation from this record.

Even so I was worried, and so was Sharff. Would Leyra, at some key moment, draw back from the record? This fear began to control our shooting schedule. We might lose weeks of work, and a large part of our production fund, if we learned too late that he would draw back from a central event. We decided to begin work with the sequence most damaging to Leyra. It was, in fact, damaging to both sides.

When the Brooklyn police began to suspect Leyra they questioned him for three days and nights with only an hour and a half of sleep during the entire period. There was also an interval during which he was allowed to attend his parents' funeral under police guard, although he was not yet technically under arrest. Except for these intervals, the questioning went on day and night, handled by relays of questioners. They hammered at him with questions about the day of the murder. He told them that on that morning he had suddenly remembered that it was his wife's birthday, and had decided to visit her in New Jersey, buying a box of candy on the way. Investigation confirmed all this. But what had he done before the New Jersey trip? The girl with whom he shared an apartment said she had gotten up early that morning, to go to work; he was still sleeping. When she saw him later that day, he seemed to be wearing a suit she hadn't seen before. It looked "brand new," she said. He also had a new raincoat. She so testified at each of the trials. Leyra told the police he had bought a new raincoat because it was raining.

They continued the questions without productive results. Leyra meanwhile began to complain of unendurable sinus pains. Finally the police said they had sent for a doctor to take care of his sinuses. A doctor arrived and took him into a room alone. The doctor, it later turned out, was a psychiatrist with a reputation for hypnotism. He had been offered a bonus if he could elicit a confession from Leyra. The proceedings were overheard by police in an adjoining room.

The doctor told Leyra he would try to help him. He would hold his hand on Leyra's forehead and they would talk quietly, to relieve his "mental tension." After a time, the police began to hear Leyra giving information he had not given before. He said that on the morning of the murder he had gone to Brooklyn and had tea with his parents. There had been a violent quarrel with his father—about the business. His father, in a fury, had left to buy a morning newspaper, planning to return immediately. The mother pleaded with Bud not to resume the argument. But Bud was likewise furious. The psychiatrist kept urging him to continue his narrative. Leyra went on haltingly, dazedly. He couldn't remember, he said. Then suddenly he asked to "speak with the captain," and was rushed back to the police, and questioning continued.

On the basis of the revelations a "confession" was typed up by the police—which, however, Leyra never signed. It said that Leyra had committed the murder in a fit of anger. It mentioned a hammer as the murder weapon. It said that Leyra had disposed of the hammer in a passing garbage truck, had gone to Manhattan, changed his clothing, and later given his blood-stained garments to a man on the street who seemed down on his luck. Then he went to New Jersey.

Leyra was formally charged. In jail he had his first meeting with the lawyer assigned to him, Frederick Scholem. During the trial Scholem began to suspect that the session with the psychiatrist had been recorded by one of the recently invented wire and tape recorders. After long legal sparring this fact was established. By court order the recording was produced and a complete transcript read into the record. It became a two-edged sword. Its contents assured Leyra's conviction. But it also showed that the doctor had led the questioning throughout. The quarrel, the hammer, and other details had been introduced not by Leyra but by the psychiatrist-hypnotist. The session included such passages as:

DOCTOR: Then you hit your mother, didn't you? With what did you hit—with a hammer? Your thoughts are coming back to you. What did you use to hit your mother with?

LEYRA: I loved my mother.

DOCTOR: I know you did. You lost your temper. Don't be afraid. A lot of people do things that they are not responsible for while in a fit of temper. You see?

LEYRA: My mother was the only thing in the world.

DOCTOR: That's right. What did you hit her with?

Minutes later:

DOCTOR: Speak up now. Speak up. See, I can make you talk very truly. I can give you an injection now. It's much better if you tell it to me this way. Come on now, speak up.

LEYRA: I can't, doctor.

DOCTOR: What kind of a hammer was it?

LEYRA: A big hammer.

DOCTOR: Was it a carpenter's hammer?

LEYRA: It was a big hammer.

DOCTOR: A big hammer. You picked it up and then what? Don't be afraid. Say it.

Still later:

DOCTOR: What did you do with the hammer—you swung it?

LEYRA: I must have, Doc. Nobody else could have done it.

DOCTOR: Nobody else could have, you say? You must have swung it?

LEYRA: I must have.

DOCTOR: And your mother fell down.

Still later:

DOCTOR: Everything is clear up to the point where you held the hammer in your hand?

LEYRA: That's right but why can't I remember from there on?

DOCTOR: If you will just stop for a moment, you will remember. And your thoughts will come into you.

LEYRA: Doctor, I am exhausted, so please be patient.

DOCTOR: I am patient.

LEYRA: I appreciate that.

DOCTOR: These people are going to throw the book at you unless you can show that in a fit of temper you got so angry that you did it. Otherwise they toss premeditation in and it's premeditation. See?... Take your time. Just relax. Want some more coffee?

LEYRA: I would like to speak with the captain.

The session lasted an hour and a half. Long passages from it were incorporated in the 1954 U.S. Supreme Court decision, and formed the basis for its dictum describing the session as "mental coercion."

Extorted confessions are barred as evidence by the laws of every state. Thus the Court ruled:

> We hold that use of confessions extracted in such a manner, from a lone defendant unprotected by counsel, is not consistent with due process of law as required by our constitution.

Sharff and I decided that the psychiatrist session must be the first item on our production schedule. We would begin with a straight-through audio enactment of passages cited by the Supreme Court. We would not photograph this reading but would record it on audiotape. The Brooklyn police declined to make the original recording available to us, but we could duplicate passages punctiliously from the transcript.

Having obtained this audio recording, we would then film the colloquy with sound, shooting short passages at a time to ease the memorization problem. We would also film shots of policemen listening in an "adjoining room," bent over a tape recorder. If Leyra should resist or flounder in our filming of any key passage, we could in those cases cut to an "adjoining room" shot, using it with a passage from the audiotape.

Attorneys for National Educational Television had constantly worried about the entire project. Fears about Leyra were eased for them when he agreed to take part, and when he and Scholem signed our sweeping release forms. But the leading NET attorney became increasingly anxious about the psychiatrist. The film could not possibly aid his professional reputation. It seemed unthinkable that he would want to participate. We were urged not to ask him: a substitute must be used, and we must not use the psychiatrist's name. Although "publication of a fair and true report of any judicial proceeding" is protected from suit under New York State civil rights law, the attorney was still nervous about the impersonation technique. In a long memorandum he pointed out that if our substitute resembled the psychiatrist, the psychiatrist could assert that his "likeness" was used without his consent. On the other hand, if there was no resemblance, he could complain that we had given a false impression of him. The memorandum continued:

> To meet this problem, I suggest that the psychiatrist and the suspect be shown as seated facing each other during the questioning and that the camera positions be such that it is the suspect's face which is seen at all times. These may be close-ups or medium shots over the psychiatrist's shoulder so that for part of the time the back of the questioner is in the foreground. Then if the questions are asked in a quiet, even, almost mechanical manner (as they probably were asked) this aspect of the production would in my opinion be justifiable.

Stefan Sharff, our director-cameraman, was delighted with this legal excursion into film technique. It was precisely how he had planned to shoot the sequence. A Columbia University speech instructor was enlisted as our "psychiatrist." Our audiotape session went with extraordinary precision, without hesitation. Then came the filming. Leyra never drew back. The same was true of all subsequent sequences.

Between shots, as lights were shifted and camera adjustments made, Leyra would sit quietly in a corner. Sharff at one time congratulated him on his patience. Leyra replied: "I've had to learn to be patient."

Leyra wanted to see the film. He had sent for his new wife to join him in New York. After the shooting they remained in the city, staying with friends in Astoria. Sharff and I meanwhile worked on the editing and narration. Gradually the film took shape.

Professor Wechsler, our consultant, came to see a rough assembly. He was pleased with the film, but dumbfounded over Leyra's decision to participate. As I recall it, Wechsler commented: "Either on the theory that he's guilty—or on the theory that he's innocent—I can't understand him doing it."

Nor could I. I felt nervous about Leyra seeing the assembled film. I was sure it would lead most viewers to assume his guilt. Yet we felt it essential to show him the film before releasing it.

I confided my anxieties to Scholem, who at once suggested a procedure. The people involved in the film should be invited to see it together in our small screening room. "You sit on one side of Bud," said Scholem, "and I'll sit on the other. As soon as it's over I'll jump up and say, 'It's great!' We'll get a sort of bandwagon going."

We adopted this embarrassing scenario. Leyra brought his new wife, a pretty redheaded lady who went by the name of Rusty. Bud and Rusty sat between Scholem and me.

Throughout the film I tried to sense any unusual motion or action by Leyra. I noticed none. At the end Scholem duly jumped up. "It's wonderful! It's really good!" Leyra got up slowly and nodded. "It's very good." Then Rusty said, "Yes, it's very good." There were handshakes and words of congratulation all around. We promised Leyra a print of the film. He and Rusty returned soon afterwards to Las Vegas.

People sometimes asked me whether I thought Leyra was guilty or innocent. I evaded the question. It was not the focus of my interest. One member of our crew asked Scholem the same question. He had a formula answer: "I didn't care whether he was guilty or innocent. If they can do that to a guilty man, they can do it to an innocent man." It seemed an effective formula. In his court presentation Scholem had suggested that the couple might have been murdered after Bud's visit, by an intruder. The Brooklyn neighborhood was regarded as "deteriorating." Scholem cited its crime rate. But in our discussions he never mentioned this argument.

The series *Decision: The Constitution in Action* won the Sylvania Award for the best educational series of 1959, as well as the Gavel Award of the American Bar Association. These awards were the result of prints submitted to award committees. People who saw it on the air must have been infinitesimal in number. The public television system, at the time the series was released, had no outlets in New York, Washington, or Los Angeles. The two dozen stations struggling to survive generally had ratings of "L. T."—meaning less than one per cent. The film reached viewers mainly through showings at conferences and film societies. I myself must have shown it dozens of times at such sessions. When I did, I was always haunted by Leyra's glazed-eye look in the interrogation scene, as he seemed truly to slip into a hypnotic trance. The psychiatrist kept at him to finish the story of the fatal morning, and Leyra could only say: ". . . . why can't I remember from there on?"

I have wondered how far that was from a possible truth —that the final moments of that morning were no longer available to his conscious mind—that they had somehow been sealed off, like a tubercular scar in the lung, firmly walled off from surrounding tissues.

Leyra, when he left New York, already had other television possibilities on his mind. He explained that one night, during his five years in Sing Sing, he had spent hours in talk with one Harry Stein, a convicted murderer who was to go to the chair next day. Stein wanted to tell him something. Stein said he had been involved in the baffling disappearance of Judge Crater, a famous unsolved mystery of August 1930. Stein told how he and others had taken the judge—who had double-crossed them after accepting a bribe—to New Jersey and dumped him in the Passaic River encased in an old bathtub. According to Leyra, Stein provided very specific details. Next day Leyra had tried to pass these on to prison guards, but they refused to listen. Leyra now said he would be glad to tell the story on television, or help reenact it. I passed the information on to one of the networks, but they decided it was not "timely." They probably assumed, in any case, that Leyra was lying. I was not sure.

I heard no news of Leyra for more than a year. Then came a long, neatly typed letter from Las Vegas.

Dear Erik:

I'll bet you will be surprised to hear from me—hope it is a pleasant surprise.

The past fourteen months have been wonderful for us, and we have enjoyed every moment. This place is fabulous. We now have a lovely home which is furnished in the best of taste and quality. We have an Oldsmobile at present, but if our good fortune continues we expect to have a pink Cadillac in the near future. I trust that dame fortune has smiled on you and yours.

Leyra mentioned that he and Rusty had bought twenty acres at Mountain Springs, Nevada, which had turned out to be rich in copper.

> ...the best prospect in the eleven western states. I am about to lease the property to a responsible group of Texan mining operators on a royalty basis. It looks as if we have hit pay dirt and that we have it made.

He was still hoping for a second television appearance, which he now thought should feature his conversations with Julius Rosenberg the night before the Rosenberg electrocution. He wondered if I knew a way to arrange it. He concluded with an invitation. "I hereby extend an open invitation to you and Stefan Sharff to visit with us at any time that would be convenient to your respective schedules. We have all modern conveniences for your comfort and it would be a pleasure to have you as our guests."

A few months later I heard from him again. He wanted me to help him write his memoirs. I was glad to be able to tell him that I was about to leave for India and would be away for at least a year. A few years later, after my return, I learned that he had died.

The film in which he appears, the seventh in the series *Decision: The Constitution in Action,* is subtitled "The Constitution and Fair Procedure." It is based on the case Leyra vs. Denno, 347 U.S. 556 (1954). Prints of the film survive in the Library of Congress, the Museum of Broadcasting and the archives of the Public Television Service. Script and correspondence are in the Columbia University Library, Special Collections.

It is still difficult to sort out one's feelings about Bud Leyra, his case, and the strange television world that brought us together. In retrospect, the case seems to belong to a moment in judicial history when concern for fair procedure burned with a special brightness. I trust it may again.

6 The Passionate Patriot

A Voice for America

PHILIP DUNNE

I take pride in the fact that once I was a propagandist. My employers were the people of the United States, and the occasion was the only truly just and truly inevitable war in our history: the war to save the world from the barbarism of Adolf Hitler. Perhaps barbarism is the wrong word. Vercingetorix and Sitting Bull, both heroic figures, could be described as barbarians. Hitler was unalloyed evil, bred in one of the world's most civilized nations.

When I first joined the U.S. Office of War Information's Overseas Branch in 1942, as chief deputy to Robert Riskin in the Bureau of Motion Pictures, I asked our overall boss, the distinguished playwright (and my long-time friend) Robert E. Sherwood, for what government bureaucrats call a policy directive. He glared down from his six-foot-seven, pointed a long finger at me, and said: "Our first policy directive is to beat the bejaysus out of Hitler, and our second is to beat the bejaysus out of Tojo. Any questions?"

No questions—but then I discovered that it wasn't quite that simple. What Bob Riskin and I were faced with was to develop a program of motion pictures, mostly documentary, which would present the United States to the world, to our allies, to neutrals, and eventually to our enemies, as the strong friend and neighbor humanity needed to defeat the racist conqueror, and then help reorder the world in peace.

There was not yet an official Voice of America, as there is today. We in the Motion Picture Bureau, along with our sister bureaus working in radio and the print media, would be the untrained, unqualified, inexperienced unofficial voice of the American people; untried attorneys, pleading America's case in the court of world opinion.

What sort of America would we present? Today's fashion seems to run to a bully nation, a land of lethal machines and high military officers laden with medals and gold braid, like their counterparts across the North Pole in the Soviet Union. It is also an America that has redefined its traditional pluralistic democracy to outlaw all economic systems but one: only entrepreneurial capitalism qualifies to operate under the rubric of democracy. Communism, of course, is anathema. If a charge of communism cannot be made to stick, we can always fall back on socialism, or Marxism, or something equally vague to stigmatize as undemocratic, and therefore as a lawful target for the overt attentions of our military, or the covert subversions of our Central Intelligence Agency.

It wasn't quite like that in 1942. We were not concerned with economic systems, pro and con, nor with adventurism or subversion. We were simply propagandists. Propagandists are salesmen, and the product we sold was human freedom.

In America, we told the world, we have our faults and foibles, just like the rest of you. But we solve our problems by using our freedoms, our democracy, as an all-purpose tool, in our politics, in our courts, in our press, in the right of our people to speak up or assemble in protest or dissent. Error can be permitted, we said (echoing Jefferson), when reason is left free to combat it.

In effect, we described America as we saw it, and as we loved it. And the America we described was not only the templed hills and waving grain of the hymns, not only the vast industrial machine, not only the military might, not only the energy of our entrepreneurs or the skills of our workers, but an intangible, poetic dream of liberty, of a free people insisting always that freedom comes first, and that, if freedom is given free play, all else will follow.

Many have articulated that dream: Walt Whitman and Mark Twain, Stephen Vincent Benet and Archibald MacLeish, Abraham Lincoln and Franklin D. Roosevelt, but none more consistently and more eloquently than Norman Corwin.

Norman was never officially a part of our OWI operation, never a registered and branded propagandist like Sherwood, Elmer Davis, John Houseman, Riskin and the rest of us, but we all knew him, and all recognized that in the work he was doing in radio and in the theater he was supplementing and even surpassing what we could do as employees of the government. He had that much more freedom, and the talent to use it.

Looking back, it seems to me now that, consciously or not, the America we officially presented was very much Norman Corwin's America.

How to describe that America? First of all, it is the America of passionate patriots, and that is a cognomen which fits Norman Corwin like a glove. Passionate patriots exhibit certain traits by which they can easily be recognized and identified.

They share a sense of history. Norman Corwin knows more American history than many who fill eminent chairs in that discipline in leading American universities. His writing is rich in history, not dragged in, as some writers drag it in, to prove his erudition, but quoted of necessity to make important points concerning our own times, and the problems that face us today and in the future. No greater problem, in my opinion, faces us at this moment than the utter ignorance of history exhibited by some who hold our very highest offices.

Passionate patriots are not afraid to criticize our leadership when they believe it is going astray. They are sometimes castigated for "blaming America first," and even for being wanting in patriotism, but only by those who confuse the nation itself and its temporary political leadership. Norman has never been afraid to criticize our leadership when he has believed it to be in the wrong, and it matters not a whit to him whether that leadership is Republican or Democratic.

The third mark of the passionate patriot, and the one most difficult for some people to understand, is that love, in the Judeo-Christian sense, what St. Paul called "charity," transcends one's own country and embraces all mankind. Richard Lovelace's gallantry to his poetical mistress: "I could not love thee, dear, so much, lov'd I not honour more," could be paraphrased: "My allegiance to my country is the firmer because I owe a greater allegiance to mankind."

This thought takes on pressing significance in the nuclear age, when blind patriotism, mindless nationalism, outright xenophobia, can lead to the destruction of our own beloved country: not only the physical land, its cities, factories and farms, not only our wonderful polyglot people, drawn from all races and continents, but the magnificent ideas which are the true heart and soul of America. Nobody understands that better than Norman Corwin. Nobody has worked harder to avert that destruction.

An America that looks out, not inward, that is generous, not mean, that is forgiving, not vengeful, that is the America we proclaimed to the world during World War II, and to which Norman Corwin has lent his mind and passion ever since. It is an America that still believes in cultivating Thomas Jefferson's "decent respect to the opinions of mankind," an America that Abraham Lincoln could describe, even in the midst of a great civil war, as a nation consecrated to government of, by, and for the people. That language was directed not to Americans alone, but to the listening world.

I am thankful, in these strident times, when the voices of hatred and unreason sound loudest in our ears, that Norman Corwin still speaks out to that same listening world.

"Though I speak with the tongues of men and angels, and have not charity, I am become as sounding brass, or a tinkling cymbal." King James's translators of the New Testament used the word "charity" not in its narrow sense of giving to the poor, but in the broader sense in which St. Paul meant the Corinthians to understand it: tolerance, respect—and love.

It is of love that Norman Corwin has always written and spoken, the love of country which will not accept for a slogan "my country, right or wrong," but only "my country, may she always be right"; the love of one's fellow human beings which is the only hope for peace in the world, perhaps for the survival of our species.

America can have no more respected, no more beloved voice. I hope that it will continue to ring out with the sound of truth in the future, as it has in the past.

7 Take a Bow

PETER DAVIS

Who can remember who made the show or who was in it? I know I can't, especially since I heard it in deep boyhood, ten or eleven, twelve at most. But there they were, I can still see them (yes, see), the two armies ranged against one another, each perched on its hill to attack, Lee against Meade, the tardy Longstreet finally weighing in against Sickles and Hancock and the other Northerners. For three long days the Southerners from Seminary Ridge battered at the Northerners defending Cemetery Ridge. We got to know boys on each side—oh, it was corny enough, the boys were probably related through a second cousin in a border state like Kentucky, and no doubt the leading Southern boy didn't really hold with slavery but thought he was fighting only to uphold states rights—and my little sister and I grimaced with pain as one of them was killed at the end of the second day. When the noble but careless General Sickles got shot in the leg and had to have it amputated, we bit down on a washcloth and pretended it was soaked in whiskey to dull the pain, and we howled as he asked to see the leg after it was taken off. We were wrenched from side to side by the throw of the drama, knowing the war was in its third year and had become madness of every kind.

The last episode left us with some thoughts, unknown in my sister's and my life up to then, unheard of in the age of television that was about to dawn and enthrone the eye over all other senses. We thought there was nobility in the idea there might be peace without victory. No narrator led us to this notion, it emerged from the radio programs we were enraptured by night after night, it grew out of the moments the actors were living. We had nothing like Bruce Catton's eloquence, just the feelings he was going to express one day. What we knew from our Zenith portable was that by July of 1863 America's tragedy was that it was caught between the absurdity of going on with the war and the impossibility, even the futility, of trying to stop it. Each side was fighting for a dreadful simplicity. Neither one could describe a solution acceptable to it without describing something wholly unacceptable to the other; neither could accept anything less than complete victory without admitting complete defeat. Both sides had heard the trumpet that would never call retreat. The peacemakers could not be heard until the sword had been sheathed; but the scabbard had been thrown away and now the Confederacy was carrying the war into the enemy's territory.

These notions floated up to us out of the Zenith on five or six successive nights, as I recall, in 1948, the conclusion of which, on the third day of Gettysburg and the final night of our own vigil, was the order given to General George E. Pickett. We couldn't stand it. My sister hid in the bathroom during a commercial but rushed back to hear the great attack down through the valley separating Seminary from Cemetery Ridge, the roar of the start of the charge giving way to the roar of shot and shell, the battle din interrupted by the whispered last words of a young Virginian to his commander, the moans of a standard-bearer cut down and handing the Stars and Bars, as his flag was labeled, to a sergeant who would try to carry it up Cemetery before the cemetery came to him. The Southern charge and Northern repulse engulfed thousands, civilization rolling itself back to hand-to-hand murder, bayonets and pummeling, mute grunts and death shrieks. Those twenty minutes of Pinkett's Charge—and they probably took about as long on the radio as they did in life and death—gave us virtually all we needed to know about war, bravery, and folly.

At this distance I have no idea whether those programs on the Civil War in the late forties were prizeworthy or critical successes or, indeed, of any lasting worth at all. I don't know if they were, in the usual sense of the word, memorable, though of course they were to me since I have remembered them. They have the force of something beyond history itself (they may have been bad, or at least cheapened history, for all I know), which is the force of dreams. That was, it seems to me, the singular contribution, the unique power, of radio. It was a medium that encouraged our visions, it elicited our fantasies instead of trapping them in tight space, instead of, as Norman Corwin has seen so sadly and beautifully, trivializing them with literalness.

Well, but why the past tense? Radio still exists, still gives us remarkable reporting in such forums as NPR's *All Things Considered,* sends us now and then an admirable drama, if only to taunt us with what things used to be like when we could hear them weekly, sometimes nightly. Thank goodness for radio's perpetuation, but it is no more, for most of us, and has long decades ago ceased to be, the medium of choice. Where it remains popular, the needle got stuck, somewhere in the 1960s, on the top forty, giving much of contemporary radio a status somewhere below wallpaper in most people's lives.

Is it possible to be grateful for the occasional excellence of television while recalling the irreplaceable virtues of radio? The struggle between the two media, obviously, is between two senses, hearing and seeing. At a glance (literally), television would seem to encompass both; surely it *uses* both, gives us sight and sound, a *son et lumiere* show that never closes down.

But the two senses, as we have seen and heard and at last understood during the decades of television's primacy, produce profoundly different effects upon us. The visual sense tyrannizes all the others. Where sight is present, it overrides the appeal to each of the remaining senses. When perfume or pizza is advertised on television, do we really almost smell or taste them? I think not, I think we are merely reminded of them, their pictures suggest a future gratification to us. Most often, the appeal of the visual is not to other senses directly but to feelings themselves: fright and hunger and Eros are perhaps the three most readily and frequently aroused. The senses of taste, touch, smell and hearing are reduced to small towns along the superhighway of sight.

Signs tell us they are there, these towns, indicators are strewn along soft shoulders and off ramps, but the quickest route to where we are headed—fear, for instance, or sexuality—is to take the bypass around the towns and stay on the interstate.

Then there is the literalness that is both the value and curse of sight. Seeing validates the other senses while it is pre-empting them—or, just as firmly, it invalidates them. Blindfolded, we may be led to touch a warm furry thing that smells invitingly kittenish. Blindfold removed, most of us will make tracks for the door when we discover we have been petting a tiger cub. Animals may scent and hear danger; for sighted humans, it remains to be seen. We may prefer another sense, we may derive more pleasure—especially if we love music—from listening, but it is our sight that saves us. Particularly in a world that places such a high value on speed, the eyes have it. A deaf cabbie is an annoyance, a blind one would be suicide. The cliche is truer every month: seeing is believing.

Where does that leave hearing? As a kind of adjunct to sight, an unobtrusive second fiddle providing background score or even "white" noise for the main event while not permitted any significance of its own? In life no, but on television, where our attention is concentrated on the small box pulsing light and imagery to the exclusion of almost everything else, the answer is yes. Life, fortunately, though still weighted in favor of sight, contains a more equal balance between the two senses, as well as opportunities —concerts, opera, lectures—for hearing to be dominant. Television, however, subordinates everything else, not only the other senses but thought itself, to what we can see. There are plenty of sounds on television, but if dialogue gets in the way of the next visual impression, technique, or trick, it has to go. When an executive tells a director to keep it moving, he means there is too much talk to listen to, not enough action to look at.

What an interesting brief time it must have been when movies were all sight, broadcasting all sound. Each could then be so much more impressionistic, heedless of the other, plunging ahead without reference to any sense but the one it owned and monopolized. It is unnecessary to be nostalgic about a pair of technologies that became as rapacious of talent, as craven to publicity and advertising as these inevitably did. But their hold on the attention of their audiences was supreme, their presence as art forms unique. Then technology lurched ahead once more, and when movies ceased to be all sight, broadcasting all sound, what was lost could never be supplied by the intended replacements. In a sense—the visual sense, that is—television did not replace radio, it replaced the old "B" movies. It filled the same void in people's lives and made use of the same actors, writers, directors, and technicians. What television did to radio, on the other hand, was push it right off the highway. As sound drove the wickedly original visual inventions off the screen, sight expelled an entire province of the imagination from broadcasting.

When in history has the sense of hearing been so elevated, so celebrated and sensitized, as it was during the reign of radio? This is when we learned, all of us who listened, that hearing has a quality not shared by any of its sensory relatives. Sound actually stimulates all the others. While the others keep to themselves, and sight in particular overwhelms the rest, hearing evokes visual images as well as smells, tastes, and physical sensations. How else could a ventriloquist be a smash hit on radio? We had to imagine Charlie McCarthy sitting next to Edgar Bergen while he insulted his presumed master and creator. To enjoy the rebellion of a son against his father—and in those days only the rebellion of a dummy could be funny and lovable—you had to be able to *see* Charlie yapping at Bergen, and radio let you do that. Could an opera singer or a stand-up monologist have become stars in silent movies? Inconceivable. And it should, by the logic of each sense appealing only to itself, being accessible only to those sensations directed solely at it, have been equally inconceivable for a ventriloquist to succeed on radio. To be dazzled or even impressed by the trick of voice-throwing you'd have to be able to see Charlie or Mortimer "talking," you'd have to be able to see that Bergen was visibly *not* talking, wouldn't you? Yes, yes, of course. But no. Bergen was as credible a vocal magician on radio as he had been in vaudeville. That was the way radio worked on you.

By appealing to all our senses, radio created a world inside of each of us. Who gets hungry watching one of Blake Carrington's banquets on *Dynasty?* We get jealous, I would submit, but not hungry, our gustatory sense is not truly engaged. Julia Child teaches us brilliantly how to cook, she doesn't make us salivate. Chef Milani did. When he got finished describing his "dinner for four, a dollar no more" you wanted that meal, no further questions asked, and you would today even if it cost twenty dollars. When one of Blake Carrington's predecessors on radio would have a banquet, you'd hear the miser licking his chops, someone else would say how delicious the food smelled, you'd get a fantastic (see Webster's: provocative of fantasy) description of caviar or beurre blanc or lobster swimming in its own juices, and depending on what city you were in you'd be ready to shoot your way into Romanoffs or "21." And yes, you'd salivate. Not with TV you won't.

The labored breathing of a wounded criminal, the throaty whisper of a woman to her lover, the whump of the Green Hornet's fist against a miscreant's jaw, the cough of Jack Benny's car trying t start, the ping of one of the Lone Ranger's silver bullets—we didn't just listen to these things the way we watch their successors on television; we inhabited their worlds and felt our way into their circumstances. Radio worked to activate our imaginations, and we worked to get inside the situations piping at us from our radios. By contrast, television is mired in the literal. At its best, television can present the world, but television never *suggests* the world. Watching TV, each of us gets the same impressions because there they are in more-or-less living color. Television is starkly unable to appeal, as radio did, to the private demons that hide in each of us, evoke the personal illusions that distinguish one of us from another. Who knew what evil lurked in the hearts of men? The Shadow did, and he's gone

Then there is money, there is *always* money. Radio could take you more places more easily and swiftly and cheaply. Whether it was the real London blitz, the imagined battle of Marathon, Napoleon marching into Russia or Hitler doing likewise, Columbus setting foot on dry land he took to be India, D'Artagnan fencing for the honor of a lady's maidenhood (no one would even have *fantasied* maidenhood then), the Bikini A-Bomb test (big as a nightmare, as it should have been, not enclosed in seventeen or nineteen blurry inches as it would be today), Caesar surrounded in the Forum, or the fateful days of Gettysburg that worked such tantalizing wonders on my sister and me, radio routinely brought us times and places quite beyond all but the most expensive broadcast specials today. A few years ago the American Bicentennial passed with very little attempt on television's part to make the revolution come alive. Period epics are simply too expensive, so history took a back seat to sitcom. That could not have happened in radio's prime. Sitcoms were all over the air in those days, as they are now, but so was history. Radio supplemented literacy, television most often supplants the literate with the literal.

Each medium has its masters. As television has had its Norman Lear, and Herbert Brodkin, Walter Cronkite and Johnny Carson, radio had its Fred Allen, Jack Benny, H.V. Kaltenborn, and Edward R. Murrow. It also had its Norman Corwin, and in the thirty-five years of television's dominance, there has been no playwright to match his vision and commitment. He learned and mastered the unique characteristics of radio until he seemed to have invented them. He took us to heroic battlefronts, taut domestic tangles, overarching moments in the lives of men and women, inside the heads of little boys, outside conventional reality to the frontiers of his art, into his own heart—and he returned us, wiser and moved, to our better selves. With his broadcasts such as *The Odyssey of Runyon Jones, We Hold These Truths, The Undecided Molecule, Murder in Studio One, My Client Curley, They Fly Through the Air,* and so many others, Corwin shaped the sensibilities of a generation. How lucky we are that when radio's tenure ended, Corwin's energy survived. Last year, in his book *Trivializing America,* he delivered to us criticisms of our mass media, our politics, and our presumed culture that have not been equaled for pure scald since Mencken. At seventy-five, he has ennobled us with his presence both anciently and recently.

Remember how Norman Corwin greeted the end of World War II? *On a Note of Triumph* came at a time when there was hope that the war we won might be followed by a peace we wouldn't lose.

So they've given up.

They're finally done in, and the rat is dead in an alley back of the Wilhelmstrasse.

Take a bow, G.I.

Take a bow, little guy.

That was how he began. We may be thankful he has not yet stopped. Wherever the best that has been expressed among us is honored his work will continue to be collected and recollected.

Now it's your turn, Norman. Take a bow.

Hear, hear.

8 It Was the Best of Times—At CBS

RICHARD J. GOGGIN

The years 1937 to 1943 were hardly the best of times for many people in America. In 1937 the depression was still being felt, Hitler was moving Germany and all of Europe toward war, and in 1939 war came. In 1941 Pearl Harbor plunged us into war, and by 1943 we were fighting fiercely in many parts of the world.

I was with the Columbia Broadcasting System in New York during those years. Looking back at my association with that network, the programs I had some involvement with, the people I met and those I worked with and for, and the "atmosphere" that pervaded 485 Madison Avenue, I recognize that for me, a young man in his early twenties, and for many colleagues of various ages, being at CBS Radio during that period in our careers was truly the best of times.

In 1937 I graduated from Manhattan College, New York with a burning desire to be an actor. Making the rounds during the day, I sought a part-time job for the evenings. I found a job as an usher at CBS. The network, having no suitable facilities at 485 for large studio audiences, had either bought or leased (I am not sure which) a number of legitimate "Broadway" theatres, constructed control rooms and viewing booths, and easily adapted the theatres into broadcast origination points, primarily for the network's popular evening radio programs. For several nights a week I ushered at these CBS Radio Playhouses for something like fifty cents an hour. In 1937 the networks were not yet in their glory in news broadcasting, but they were riding high in entertainment broadcasting in a variety of program types and formats.

The memories of some of the sponsored shows originating at the CBS Playhouses still remain fresh: among them the DuPont *Cavalcade of America,* the Phil Baker quiz show for Gulf Oil, the Philip Morris program and Johnny, the *Kate Smith Hour,* and an evening "soap" called *Second Husband,* with Helen Mencken and Jay Jostyn.

Of these once-a-week programs, the one I perhaps remember best was the *Ben Bernie* show which originated in the small theatre at the top of the New Amsterdam Building on West 42nd Street. I was assigned to work the show's rehearsal and air-time periods as a kind of go-fer for Ben, his secretary, Eleanor, the band leader, Al Evans, and the two writers, Parke Levy and Al Miller. (Decades later, when I was chairman of television, motion pictures, and radio at New York University, we hired Al Miller to teach for us.) The *Ben Bernie* show was my first real opportunity to get close to the inner workings of a professional radio program and its production. It was this experience, I think, that began to change my career goals from acting to production.

In the late 1930's CBS had in operation an apprentice training program, centered in the network Program Department. The apprentices were recent college graduates who were hired for a period of a year (at $25.00 a week), and who were assigned to different CBS departments to learn about programs and production. If the apprentices proved promising during the trial year, one or more would be given permanent jobs. The Personnel Department, under Joseph Burgess, did the initial screening of applicants and then the likely ones were interviewed by the higher-ups. I applied in 1938, while still an usher, one of four hundred applicants for the four openings in the 1938–39 group.

I clearly remember being interviewed by William B. Lewis, the vice-president in charge of programs; Douglas Coulter, his second in command; Max Wylie, head of the Script Department; Frank Barton, in charge of the Program Service and Ideas Department; and Frank Stanton, head of Research. Those finally selected were Bill Murphy, Phil McHugh (now Chairman of McHugh and Hoffman, the broadcasting consulting firm), Peter Steele (the son of the short story writer, Wilbur Daniel Steele), and me.

The four of us started out that summer of 1938 with Frank Barton. CBS was constantly receiving program ideas, not only from professional sources but also a great many unsolicited ideas from people all over the country. The submissions (sometimes scrawled in pencil or pen) ran the gamut from simple one-page letters to elaborate presentations. We apprentices read and evaluated them, but we obviously had no power to accept or reject. We also helped prepare program presentations that CBS was making to advertising agencies and sponsors. As initial exposure and training the experience was invaluable.

We spent several weeks in the Research Department learning something about the fundamentals of audience research and measurement from Harper Carraine, Oscar Katz, and Charles Smith. From then on the apprentices worked separately rather than as a group.

During the fall, winter, and spring of 1938–39 I seem to have worked back and forth between the Script Department and the Production Department. The Program Department, on the 18th floor at 485 Madison, was the creative center of CBS. Here, in what would seem now to be a rather small area, were the offices of executives, administrators and the producers, directors and writers: Bill Lewis, Douglas Coulter, Davidson Taylor (who supervised important sustaining programs), Eleanor Inman (religious programs), Al Rinker (who produced popular music programs), Lucille Singleton (who auditioned singers), Gerald Maulsby, Roy Passman and Allan Parr (program operations), Marge Morrow (casting), and Nila Mack (of children's programs and *Let's Pretend* fame). Helen Sioussat (talks) may have had her office there also.

The Script Department was there, with Max Wylie and the writers William H. Fineshriber, Margaret Lewerth, and Charles R. Jackson (who later wrote *The Lost Weekend*). And, of course, the directors: Norman Corwin, Earle McGill, Brewster Morgan, William N. Robson, and George Zachary. Not all of them had their offices on the 18th floor, but the directors' presence was felt no matter where they were located.

Many of these people, particularly the creative ones, had only to be concerned with and focussed upon the very special world of CBS-produced sustaining programs. They were, in a very real sense, pleasantly isolated from "commercial" broadcasting. There wa no need for them to care much about the sponsored programs on the network schedule. Most of the sponsored programs wer wholly produced by advertising agencies, with the networks providing little more than air time, facilities, research, and promotion. They were not privy to the administrative problem and strategies of the 20th floor executives, President William S. Paley, Executive Vice President Edward Klauber, and Vice-President Lawrence Lowman. The creative people had no involvement in the struggle for sales and maximum audiences, and they were remote from the stress of inter-network competition and the frustration of dealing with the federal government and its agencies. As Eric Barnouw wrote in *The Tower in Babel* "The happily insulated compartments of network operation ha a sheltering effect."

CBS was not located in a glamorous setting like NBC was in Radio City. CBS was in an undistinguished office building, 485 Madison Avenue, at the corner of 52nd St., and unrelated businesses occupied many of the floors. The CBS initials were on the marquee, but there was no ticket booth in the small lobby and there were no studio tours. The overall appearance was far fron imposing, yet there was magic in coming to work there each da Even now the words "485 Madison" bring me pleasure much as they brought excitement well over forty years ago. CBS is long gone from Madison Avenue; it moved west to Sixth Avenue an into its own new and special building, not too lovingly referred to as Black Rock. I have no ties to, no investment in that huge edifice. CBS became institutionalized and broadcasting itself has changed. But for me CBS will always be 485 Madison Avenue, for there everything was smaller, more intimate, more personal. I think I was there at the right time.

Today the networks' television schedules are filled with sponsored programs almost from one end of the broadcast day to the other. But the same networks in my time, in radio, had a great many hours during the day and late evening when the schedules showed solely "sustaining," unsponsored, in-house produced programs. These were fed from New York out to the owned an the affiliated stations as part of the networks' contractual obliga tion to supply their affiliates with a certain number of program hours each week. Many of these sustainers were important, prestige programs of drama, serious music, talks, special events, news, and religion. The bulk, however, was likely to be fifteen-minute or half-hour programs of popular music, featuring contract musicians, such as organists Fred Feible and Charles Paul, or contract singers such as Buddy Clark, Edith Dick, Audrey Marsh, and Barry Wood.

There were small instrumental ensembles and full orchestras, playing popular or serious music, led by CBS staff conductors Howard Barlow, Ray Bloch, Bernard Herrmann, Lyn Murray, Raymond Scott and his brother, Mark Warnow.

On script assignments I sat at a desk in the passageway outside Charley Jackson's office and composed continuity for several hundred popular music broadcasts, struggling each day to find variants of "And now we hear...." (Bill Fineshriber wrote the more prestigious classical music programs.) Nonetheless it was fun and a bit of a challenge. I did enjoy writing some of the variety programs that Mark Warnow and Ray Bloch presented and following through in the studio, rehearsing the announcer if the script was upbeat and playful (Bert Parks was particularly adept at this).

I recall one very satisfying writing assignment: I researched and scripted a program for the News and Special Events Department about the total lunar eclipse of November 7, 1938. We had two-way communication between Bob Trout on the roof of 485 and Charles Stark reporting from a TWA plane flying over Manhattan Island. Also on board the plane were Trubee F. Davison, President of the American Museum of Natural History, and William H. Barton, Jr., the Executive Curator of the Hayden Planetarium. Professor Barton, a most pleasant, helpful, and learned man, was our resource expert and special commentator for the broadcast.

One other special script assignment I well remember: In the early spring of 1939, CBS had no commercial program to schedule against NBC in the key time slot of 8–9 P.M. on Sundays. The Program Department decided to build a big, relatively large-budget musical-variety sustaining series to put in that hour, and to have it originate in one of the CBS Playhouses before a large audience. The series producer was Al Rinker, one of the original Rhythm Boys with Bing Crosby, a time in his life that Al never forgot. H and Dave Taylor chose me to write the scripts. The series starte off with Hoagy Carmichael as Host, but he was Host only for the first show, on March 26, 1939. After that Dan Seymour toc over as Master of Ceremonies. The programs featured performers prominent on the popular music scene, among them being Mildred Bailey, Raymond Scott and his small group, the Alec Wilder Octet, and the John Kirby Trio, together with Ray Bloch and the CBS house orchestra. A small disaster happened durin one broadcast when John Kirby (his Trio was the closing act) misunderstood a signal and didn't play the long version of his final number. The show wound up at least a minute short and we had to play an untold number of choruses of the theme, "Cheek to Cheek"—it seemed it would never end.

After several broadcasts it became apparent that what I was scripting and what Al Rinker wanted didn't match. I dropped the writing, bu continued on as Al's production assistant. So much for ups and downs at the typewriter.

The most exciting experiences were related to my several months in the Production Department. All CBS programs from New York, commercial or sustaining, had assigned to them CBS engineers and production men. The latter functioned in several capacities They acted as CBS production representatives on commercial shows (which almost invariably had outside producers, directors, and announcers), as assistant directors to network Program Department producers and directors on a larger sustaining shows, and as *de facto* directors for lesser sustaining programs that were not complex or important enough to have network producers or directors.

We apprentices wrote programs and functioned as production men for sustaining programs. To my knowledge the staff writers raised no objection to this, but a few of the older production men did. Their sense of territory seemed greater. Some previous years' apprentices, among them Guy della Cioppa, Rolf Kaltenborn, and Jack Mosman, had been promoted to full-status productio men, and their presence eased the situation. Further, the 21st floor Production Office, with John Carlisle, Jack Stapp, Dick Linkroum, Bob Ray, and Jim Brown, was very supportive.

The other production men whose friendliness was appreciated and from whom we learned were Robert Emerson, Harry Frazee, Orry Hancock, Larry Harding, Paul LaPorte, Betsy Tuthill (the only woman), and Ted Wick. (The reputed starting salary for production men was $50.00 a week; it was said that at CBS-Los Angeles the salary was only $35.00 a week—but everyone knew that out there the livin' was easy.)

The apprentices were assigned almost exclusively to sustaining programs. As a production man (in effect, if not by Personnel Department classification), I worked the range of smaller programs for which I had previously written scripts, "directing" them with assists from staff announcers and engineers. Among the staff announcers then were George Bryan, Harry Clark, Larry Elliott, James Fleming, Frank Gallup, Tony Marvin, Bert Parks, David Ross, Charles Stark, and Niles Welch. Among the engineers were John Dietz, Harry Hicks, Jack Mason, Ted Miller, Joe Travis, Van Vorhes, and Paul Wittlig.

I worked also on some larger sustaining programs, such as *What Price America?*, *Americans at Work,* and *Let's Pretend.* Occasionally I was assigned as second production man on commercial shows, among them *Gangbusters,* directed by Harry Frazee, *99 Men and a Girl,* featuring Hildegarde and a huge orchestra conducted by Raymond Paige, *The Lucky Strike Hit Parade,* and *The Major Bowes Capitol Family.*

From time to time there were production assignments on the broadcasts of the News and Special Events Department, so ably run by Paul White, who seemed to this youngster to be a gruff and unapproachable man. What a lineup of journalistic talent and skillful correspondents he and Edward Klauber and Edward R. Murrow built up in White's Department then and in the war years to come: Cecil Brown, Winston Burdett, Charles Collingwood, Elmer Davis, Bill Downs, Richard Hottelet, H. V. Kaltenborn, Larry Lesueur, Eric Sevareid, William L. Shirer, and Bob Trout. Everyone in broadcasting then will remember *The CBS World News Roundup* that started in March, 1938. The News Room and offices were in a small area of the 17th floor, but from that space and in those difficult years of crucial global events CBS did a magnificent job of informing America.

There were remote broadcasts also: *American School of the Air,* for instance, originated sometimes from a gymnasium in a public school, *The Gospel Singer* with Edward McHugh came from the Aeolian organ studio on Fifth Avenue, and there were the late-hour popular dance band pick-ups from night spots in hotels or places like the The Meadowbrook in New Jersey where Woody Herman was playing. (I remember those nights travelling back and forth to New Jersey in a station wagon full of CBS gear and driven by the taciturn engineer, Harry Hicks).

In addition to our assignments, we apprentices haunted 485's studios and the Playhouses, watching rehearsals and broadcasts of both sustaining and commercial programs. In the process of our unstructured education we absorbed and grew: we learned about microphones and their patterns, about orchestra and microphone placement, the characteristics of musical instruments, acoustics, audio balancing and mixing, sound effects and music effects, program timing, rehearsal techniques, and directing. We never had a lecture, a class session, a prescribed reading list, or an examination. It was learn by watching and doing, an immensely practical approach.

At one time in 1939 I was "lent" to CBS Television to help set up their recorded music library. CBS-TV then occupied a large, high, open area at 15 Vanderbilt Avenue in the vast reaches of Grand Central station. At opposite ends of this space were the large control room and the offices; in the middle was the studio. Leonard Hole was the main executive, Gilbert Seldes was in charge of programming, assisted by Ruth Norman, and Phil Goetz was the chief engineer; there was a cadre of engineers and production people who have been referred to, not unkindly, as the "Seven Old Men," which they were not.

Being in television then was like being a member of a secret society; most broadcasting people asked, with radio booming, why would anyone want to work in television? There were only a meagre number of program hours on the air at WCBW, the usual assortment of program material that characterized the early days of experimental television—dance, puppets, magicians, interviews, short films, and some short live plays. I was an assistant floor manager on several live programs, including that old chestnut, *The Monkey's Paw.*

Television transmissions in those days were in black and white, but very early in the 1940's Peter Goldmark and his research group of engineers gave a demonstration for CBS personnel of mechanical color television. The colors were clear, well-defined, and vivid. It was impressive. When Hitler attacked Poland and the war started in Europe, CBS, as I recall, shut down its television program operations and WCBW confined its transmissions to engineering testing.

The evening of Sunday, October 30, 1938 was undoubtedly one of the strangest times I have ever spent in a radio or television studio. Early that evening I was in a small transcription studio on the 23rd floor, next to Master Control. By 7:30 P.M. I had finished the production of a transcribed music program that had been short-waved to South America. CBS was originating such broadcasts as part of a U.S. Government contract (John Hundley produced the programs). About 7:45 P.M. I entered Studio One on the 22nd floor and crossed to what was called the sub-control room, a small viewing and listening space for guests, connected to the studio control room. Looking out through the double windows, one saw the bustling activity of actors, musicians, and sound-effects technicians, a not-at-all unusual scene in the last minutes before air time.

On a small platform at the epicenter of all this, music stand with script in front of him, earphones banded around his head, shirt open at the throat, dark hair in disarray, eyes gleaming, red-hot, was the director, Orson Welles. The program that night was to be *The War of the Worlds.*

The broadcast started out normally enough with appropriate credits (which, unfortunately, vast numbers of listeners missed) to Orson Welles and *The Mercury Theatre on the Air,* and to H. G. Wells' novel, and then proceeded leisurely into the opening dramatization. Not too long after came the series of "news interruptions" of the "program"— perhaps annoying or puzzling at first, but not alarming. But in time the "interruptions" took over, and alarm and fright spread across the nation, caused by the terrifying event that was happening that night in the vicinity of Grovers Mill, New Jersey and being reported to listeners over the CBS network.

Three other people besides me were in the sub-control room; if my memory is accurate, they were the actor, Vladimir Sokoloff and his wife, and Welles' wife, Virginia. As the dramatization became more vivid, Mrs. Sokoloff turned to Mrs. Welles and said, "If I were listening at home now, I would be terribly frightened by this." I looked askance at her—it's only a play, I said to myself. How wrong I was. Suddenly the telephones began ringing in the control room; one telephone was linked to the main switchboard and the other directly to Master Control. Telephones in control rooms were never used during live broadcasts unless there was an emergency. There was certainly one that night. We could hear the raised voices in the control room, and then the CBS production man came out of it, hurried past us, and went out into the studio to confer. Tension was becoming enormous in Studio One. They had a tiger by the tail and could do little but hang on to the end. There were two subsequent announcements about the broadcast being a dramatization, once announcement before and one after the middle break, plus the closing announcement by Orson Welles saying it was only a Halloween prank. But the middle break was quite late, coming well after the half-hour mark, and the damage had already been done.

We tumbled out of the studio at 9 P.M. to find telephones ringing furiously in the reception area. The switchboard operators, overwhelmed by the deluge of incoming calls, were patching them through to any place at 485 where there might be people to answer them. We all did, trying to explain to, placate, and assure frightened and angry listeners. One outraged caller asked me who was the President of CBS; I told him and he replied, "Tomorrow I'm inviting him to a funeral. My wife just died." I don't remember how I responded; I was too dumbfounded.

CBS gave support to its sustaining dramatic programs, the more prestigious ones in particular. Because of my interest in theatre I gravitated naturally to them. The "soaps" and other sponsored dramatic programs were in the main well done technically. For me, however, they had little or none of the appeal of CBS' sustaining dramatic programs which originated in the network Program Department, and which were produced and directed with intelligence, imagination and style by Norman Corwin,

Earle McGill, Brewster Morgan, Irving Reis, William N. Robson, and George Zachary. No routine productions for these men, if they could help it; rather, they sought out the different idea, the unusual story, the challenging structure that would allow and even demand experimentation.

Irving Reis, formerly a CBS radio engineer, led the way, writing and directing *Meridian 7-1212* among others, and creating what became in July, 1936 the renowned *Columbia Workshop.* I arrived too late at CBS and missed him, but I was there for the others. I recall being in the control room for Zachary's fine production on July 23, 1938 of T. S. Eliot's *Murder in the Cathedral.* Most *Columbia Workshop* productions were one-half hour in length and were produced in Studio One. This production ran a full hour and originated in Liederkranz Hall in Manhattan, which CBS had equipped with studio facilities mainly for serious music programs.

I never worked with Brewster Morgan, but I did occasionally with Earle McGill. He was a jovial man, much liked by actors and technicians, a careful craftsman and a skillful director whose productions were always first rate. He directed most of the *American School of the Air* programs, many of which were written, I believe, by Margaret Lewerth. I watched and admired the *Columbia Workshop* production Earle did on August 6, 1938 of Stephen Vincent Benet's *The Devil and Daniel Webster.* Charley Jackson dramatized it for radio, and the music was conducted by Bernard Herrman.

I was drawn magnetically to the studios of two CBS directors, Norman Corwin and William N. Robson, because of the subject matter and production values of their programs, and because of Norman's and Bill's creativity and personalities.

Bill Robson exuded theatricality—even in his attire, often wearing a cape and a green Tyrolean hat, not the usual garb at 485 Madison. I think it was in 1936 that Bill Lewis brought him to CBS from station KHJ, Los Angeles. When Reis left CBS, Robson became the chief director of the *Columbia Workshop.* He did a lot of radio writing in his long career, but drama direction was his forte, and he loved it. The studio and control room were his territory. He was always in complete control of the elements of production, and the more complicated they were, the better. He attacked his scripts; they were things to wrestle with and conquer. Actors and technicians worked hard for him, both becaus they liked him and because he knew what he wanted. A musician himself, he was tremendous on the use of music for mood and character. He also had a keen ear for the precise and well-done sound effect.

I remember with pleasure being present at three particular productions of Bill's. The first was the May 28, 1938 broadcast of *Bury the Dead,* the play by Irwin Shaw that Bill adapted for radio and directed with flair and energy. Later, on December 29,1938, he directed another *Columbia Worshop* production *Crosstown Manhattan.* An "experiment in American documentary broadcasting," it was written by Travis Ingham and included "a verse picture of Broadway" written especially for the program by Norman Corwin. The orchestra was conducted by Mark Warnow. The broadcast took the listener on an inspired journey across 52nd Street from the East River to the Hudson River; the "characters" and the vignettes, and the sound and music patterns were wonderful.

I assisted Bill on several of his productions, sometimes editing scripts, setting music cues, occasionally casting shows with Marge Morrow—in addition to the usual routine of a production man.

The third production of Bill's that I keenly remember, and on which I worked, was the December 31, 1938 hour-long "annual year's end broadcast" of the CBS Special Events Department, called *Twelve Crowded Months.* Many newsworthy events happened in 1938: The great hurricane of September that ravished the Northeast, the Anschluss of Nazi Germany and Austria, Howard Hughes' flight around the world in ninety-one hours, Wrong-Way Corrigan's solo flight to Ireland, the controversial Wage-Hour legislation, the Sino-Japanese War, the Nazi takeover of the Sudetenland, the Musica-Coster-McKesson and Robbins scandal, the shooting in Paris of Ernst vom Rath, and the consequent bloodlust and hate against the Jews in Germany and that second great "hurricane," in October of 1938, *The War of the Worlds.*

These news events were dramatically re-created in *Twelve Crowded Months* in the form quite typical of American documentary radio of that era. The script was writen mainly by Travis

Ingham, John Lagemann, and Bill Robson. I wrote the Ernst vom Rath and part of the Wage-Hour sections. I assisted Bill in editing the overall script, but it was he who did the rewrites and who gave the script its final polish. On the first page of my production copy of the script he wrote "To the guy who in a very material sense made this script possible—Bill Robson to Dick." His appreciation of a rank beginner meant a great deal to me.

Paul White supervised the broadcast, Frank Gallup was the Narrator, and Bernard Herrmann conducted the orchestra. It was a difficult and complicated production, demanding weeks of preparation. Bill directed it with his customary skill and verve, just two days after directing *Crosstown Manhattan*! It was all an exhilarating experience for me.

The outstanding radio programs of the thirties and forties could not have been as outstanding as they were without the availability of a whole corps of talented actors. There were two kinds of actors then—or perhaps two kinds of attitudes. There were those actors in New York who thought of themselves as theatre actors and who, if they acted in radio at all, acted not by choice but mainly because of the very practical need for actors at any time to have some source of income besides the theatre. There were other actors who had a more committed feeling toward radio, even though many of the commercial programs they appeared on required not much more than minimal, even stock performances. But the best of these actors could look forward to being cast from time to time in experimental programs at 485 Madison and Radio City and to working with exciting directors.

Among the gifted actors and actresses whom I observed were Ray Collins, Don Costello, Kenneth Delmar, Ted di Corsia, Reynolds Evans, Betty Garde, House Jameson, Ed Jerome, Adelaide Klein, Ed Latimer, Frank Lovejoy, Agnes Moorehead, Arnold Moss, Santos Ortega, Guy Repp, Luis van Rooten, Everett Sloane, Robert Straus, and Dwight Weist. The list could go on.

Sometime in the spring, I believe, of 1938 Bill Lewis heard Norman Corwin's poetry programs over WQXR in New York and brought him to CBS. It was one of the best decisions Bill Lewis ever made. Norman, then in his late twenties, was a handsome, quiet, and even reserved man. From what I observed of him he went about his writing and directing with a minimum of fuss, calmly and surely revealing the great talent he was bringing to the medium of radio.

Norman, in the winter of 1938, introduced *Words Without Music,* his weekly experimental series in which initially he adapted and dramatized other peoples' works. I was a production man on the program he did on January 22, 1939, based on his unique treatment for radio of Carl Sandburg's *The People, Yes.* Through voices, choruses of voices, rhythm, timing, and manipulation of text Norman brought added distinctiveness to Sandburg's words. There was music on this program, composed and performed on the organ by Charles Paul. It was a fascinating program to hear and to watch.

Norman's original radio verse-drama, *They Fly Through the Air with the Greatest of Ease,* was first done on the *Words Without Music* series. I watched it in the studio when he repeated it on April 10 1939, for the *Columbia Workshop.* The opening lines of the script read, "The author dedicates this poem to all aviators who have bombed defenseless civilian populations, and machine-gunned helpless refugees." His script was a moving and deeply felt expression of dismay at the inhumanity of man to man. As a production it was extremely effective; it still has meaning for today and could well be repeated every year.

House Jameson was the Narrator. The audio control was by John Dietz, a creative engineer who was great to work with and whose services were much sought after when important and difficult programs were to be done. The sound-effects were well performed by Ray Kramer and John McClusky (they, along with Joe Gratz, Ora Nichols, and Vic Ruby, were excellent sound-effects technicians at CBS).

Sometime in the 1938–39 season Norman produced and directed a fifteen-minute, five-a-week, early evening series that was called, I think, *County Seat.* It was the simple story of a pharmacist in a small town, written by Milton Geiger, who was himself a pharmacist before he wrote professionally. The program originated in the Seventh Avenue studios of Columbia Records, and I was production man on it several times.

Of all of Norman's programs that I have heard over the years, one of the very earliest still has a special significance for me—*The Plot to Overthrow Christmas.* It may have been his first original script for CBS, and I had the great good fortune to be the production man on that Christmas Day of 1938 when it was first heard. It was a happy occasion to be in the control room with Norman, to watch him direct the actors and sound-effects men, and to hear his delighted chuckles as the quietly funny rhymes and jokes and word play came alive off the pages of the script. On the title page of my production copy is written. "To Dick Goggin—whose help to me made the show easy to get across—Norman Corwin." I doubt that I made any significant contribution, but his generous comment pleased me very much.

The actors that day were Eric Burroughs as Nero, House Jameson as Santa Claus, Will Geer as the Devil, Don Costello as the Sotto Voce person, Arnold Moss as the Narrator and Simon Legree, Neil O'Malley as Ivan the Terrible, Lucille Meredith as Miss Borgia, Robert Straus as Haman, and Sydney Smith as the Courtier. At the program's end Norman stepped to the microphone to say to the listeners that he hoped they "liked our little demonstration today of the Triumph of Good over Evil" and to wish them "a very Merry Christmas and the happiest of New Years." It was a wonderful way for all of us in the studio to have spent Christmas Day.

Norman was a highly accomplished director. It was intensely interesting to me to watch him at work in the studio, to note his unfailing courtesy to his cast and technical crew and to see how they responded with admiration and respect, to sense that he was both leading them and testing himself in the service of the script. Through all his experimentation, and with his great skill in creating interweaving patterns of voice, music, and sound effects—and silence, Norman with his productions helped deepen and enrich the concept of radio drama as The Theatre of the Imagination.

Yet for all my appreciation of him as a producer and director, I think of Norman basically as a writer and poet, and this I suspect is what he would most want to be remembered for. Obviously, all during his long career he has had a love affair with the English language. Like some conjurer of old he can take words and put them together so that they illuminate our minds, touch our eyes and hearts, nudge our intellect, and challenge our conscience. I continue to be awed by his productivity and amazed at its range and quality.

Norman Corwin was and is an original. There has never been anyone else quite like him in the entire history of American broadcasting.

In summer, 1939, shortly before my apprenticeship would have been over, CBS offered me a regular position. To some extent I left the network scene to becomes a writer-producer-director in the Program Department WABC, New York (now WCBS), CBS' flagship station. But that is another story.

Those first years of 1937–39 were pretty heady stuff for a young man in his early twenties. One was—in New York and at CBS—in the center of broadcasting, and lucky enough to be in a stimulating environment, rubbing elbows and working with some of radio's most talented people. It was a very special way to start out on a career in broadcasting.

Some years later, Ben Feiner said to me, "Every once in a while CBS rolls over on its young." Perhaps there are some who, from their own experience, might agree. Happily, it didn't happen to me. Those five-and-one-half years of my life, at CBS, could not have been better spent. They were for me truly the best of times.

Who Knows Who May Be Listening? And Where?

JEROME LAWRENCE

On April 24, 1939 (and quite a few times afterwards) a poetic panegyric to the art and wonder of broadcasting, in the author's words "commingled with northern lights and asteroids and Alexander's skeleton." It was a landmark radio play in verse, Norman Corwin's *Seems Radio's Here to Stay.* Its closing lines were:

Here is a thought to fasten to your throat:
Who knows who may be listening? And where?

In the forty-five years since, television has inundated our living rooms, inviting us to turn on its channels and turn off our imaginations. We can't help wondering: was Norman overly sanguine about the permanence of this man-and-God-made miracle? Has radio's limitless, unfettered theatre-of-the-mind disappeared forever?

Hell, no.

Is it too fanciful to believe that every voice, every sound, every bar of music ever broadcast still lingers in the air? Those vibrations must still be out there, waiting for us to tune them in: FDR and Allen's Alley; Edward R. Murrow and Baby Snooks; the electric excitement of VJ-Day and the inspired zaniness of Gracie Allen; Toscanini and Spike Jones.

Or perhaps some distant planet has just invented radio or perfected those great listening devices, ears and minds, and our sound waves are just reaching their shores. They hear a baby-cry in a radio play and must think it is the birth of a whole new civilization. (It would in fact be Jerry Hausner, gurgling into a handkerchie with his acting expertise out-gurgling any baby ever born.)

We have stood on a spit of land jutting out into the unpacific Pacific and stared into the eyepiece of Philip Dunne's incredible telescope. We've gasped at the rings of Saturn, the moons of Jupiter, pondered star-clusters, galaxies, nebulae millions of light years away. The diamond-light is just reaching our eyes. We believe i the equal permanence of waves of creative thoughts, broadcast from radio transmitters, broadcast from thinking minds. We have a lyric in one of our stage musicals:

Every thought ever thought
Is as lasting as time.

We still hear them, loud and clear: words, ideas, music, flights of imagination. They still fill the air. We're still listening.

The eight-year-old son of a friend of ours was confined to a dark room recently because of measles. He was deprived of the glaring lig of his all-demanding, ever-present babysitter, television. His devoted father arranged for a tape player and broadcasts of some radio plays, including Corwin's *My Client Curley* and *Th Odyssey of Runyon Jones* and the Columbia Workshop produc tion of our *Inside a Kid's Head.* When the measles had disappeared, the eight-year-old announced: "I like radio more than I do television."

"Oh?" his father said. "And why is that?"

"The pictures are so much better," the boy glowed, with more light and enlightenment coming out of his face than from the brightest television tube.

There is literature of radio which *must* be preserved, rebroadcast, not merely in the pages of the all-too-few published volumes of broadcast scripts. We'd like to make a Modest Proposal to Pub Radio, to the networks and their affiliates. The great operas go into the repertory of the world's opera houses; the great plays continue to be revived in playhouses everywhere. Why should current and future generations be deprived of the gems of radio?

We propose not a look-back, but a "listen-back"—on the air 52 weeks a year, regularly, annually. Ideally, they should be the original transcriptions of the live broadcasts. In some instances, new productions could be arranged. Anybody interested? We'll make you a list, which will include at least a dozen Corwins (certainly *Untitled* and *The Plot to Overthrow Christmas* every December 24 or 25 from here on). Arch Oboler must loom large, including James Cagney in the brilliant radio play Oboler fashioned from Dalton Trumbo's *Johnny Got His Gun;* Bette Davis as Mme. von Meck and Hans Conreid as Tchaikovsky in *This Lonely Heart* on Screen Guild Theatre. Several of Orson Welles' Mercury Theatres should be part of this thundering cavalcade, certainly the broadcast of Conrad's *Heart of Darkness.* (Anybody who wrote for Welles said that his cello-voice could "dignify a comma") Pick any of Morton Wishengrad's scripts from *The Eternal Light* (a noteworthy weekly program on Jewish subjects) or any of Ranald MacDougall's radio documentaries from *Man Behind the Gun* (a dynamic series which penetrated the minds of World War II fighting men.)

Archibald MacLeish's *Fall of the City* should be heard, year after year, by young ears. Theatre Guild of the Air gave us brilliant dramatizations by the then-unknown Arthur Miller, Robert Anderson, John Patrick. Arthur Laurents should be included; one of his scripts from *Assignment Home* (the problems of returning servicemen) would still sear the airwaves. Irving Reis, who founded Columbia Workshop, wrote and directed one of the most innovative of the early experimental broadcast-dramas, *Meridian 7-1212;* it must not be forgotten. And we are perhaps without humility to suggest that some of Lawrence and Lee's radio productions be included: Vincent Price, Betsy Blair, and Elliot Lewis in *Mr. Shakespeare,* John Huston and Jeff Corey in *The Maniac,* Lurene Tuttle giving the performance of her life in *The Glass Eye.* Or may we suggest one or two of the 299 musicals we did on The Railroad Hour, possibly *Penny Whistle,* about

Robert Louis Stevenson. Our D-Day broadcast (with Corwin as Narrator), *Lord Haw-Haw Will Not Be Heard Tonight* might appropriately be listened to each June.

Note that most, if not all, of the writers listed here became playwrights for the stages of Broadway and the world. Radio was their workshop (Columbia and elsewhere) and they learned to make words and language dance.

Note, too, that Broadway playbills, listing the literary credits of these playwrights, rarely printed the fact that they had written for radio. Perhaps the elitist attitude of the theatre, particularly the critics, decried that anything that sprang from a mass medium must be junk, trash, pulp, penny-dreadful, soap-opera drivel. How wrong they were.

We ourselves were fortunate enough never to be trapped in the treadmill of writing for the "soaps," though once, in the clutches of penury, I wrote one episode (on a battered Underwood in a cold-water flat in Manhattan) and shipped it off to the Minneapolis advertising agency. Back came this wire, which I have kept as a "never again, never since" warning to myself:

You can't kidnap a baby on NBC.
Can you make it a dog or something?

I did have one other personal encounter with the daytime soap operas. While on staff at CBS, I was assigned to listen to as many as I could over a period of a month to try to analyze what made the high-rating ones work. After a month of perpetual emotion, I came up with this conclusion: *All the women suffer and all the men are heels.* Watching the "Prime-Time Soaps" on television these days will convince you that the formula still applies.

Goodman Ace, who wrote a witty and memorable daytime-strip, *Easy Aces,* had a similar theory: "Just think of a story which contains romance or finance. As for me, there are weeks when I can't think of one for love or money."

Goody wrote that for a book we put together: *Off Mike* (Duell, Sloan & Pearce, 1944), a compendium of words-of-wisdom by the working radio writers of the time. Alas, it is out-of-print, but it contained chapters of infinite help to peers and neophytes by Corwin, Oboler, Ace as well as: Gertrude Berg, True Boardman Abe Burrows, Ranald MacDougall, Nila Mack, Bill Morrow,

Carlton E. Morse, Don Quinn, Sherwood Schwartz, Everett Tomlinson, Bob Welch, and George Wells. Robert E. Lee, the "Nostradamus of Television," even wrote a chapter on "Writing for Video" some years before there was any video to write for.

Several passages from *Off Mike* might be pertinent, forty-one years later. From Norman Corwin's chapter:

"If I were to suggest any tactics they would be those recommendable to any artist in any medium—the pursuit of the sane life and the good cause, the unceasing search for knowledge of the world and the truth of its issues, a striving for simplicity and directness, a curiosity about Man and his ways. These are the large things, these are the endless quests."

As editor of *Off Mike,* I gave this closing advice to beginning writers. And to myself.

"Writing is very much like being in love. It has to be a projection of your own particular and distinctive brand of charm, intelligence, integrity, and general attitude toward life. If the chemistry that brings those things out is gone, the honeymoon's over.

"A friend of mine, while in the weary punch-drunk state that most radio-writers get into around 3:00 A.M. on a deadline night, once said: 'Every good writer has the inalienable right to stink occasionally.' Let us not relax on such a thought, brothers. Let's stink as seldom as possible.

"Tomorrow has a good chance of being just about the best tomorrow the world has ever seen. To chart that bright day belongs in the hands of the literate, the articulate, the men and women who can crystallize thoughts into words, who can boil down the mass hope and fill the air with it in loud and clear tones.

"In our plays, in our commentaries, yes, in our jokes too, we can say the important things. We can point the way. We can help build the future."

Were we overly idealistic? Perhaps. But we were convinced that somebody was listening.

Somewhere.

Still.

10 Profits of Doom

James A. Brown

The Golden Age of Radio (the late 1930s to the end of the 1940s) differed in many ways from our own Brass Age of Television. Then, the still-developing regulations by the Federal Communications Commission emphasized radio's role in serving the cultural and informational interests of the American public. In the earliest years, broadcast leaders such as David Sarnoff and other entrepreneurs were loathe to sully their broadcast companies' programs, reaching out through the night air into people's homes, with specific mention of prices and overly commercial or otherwise indiscreet advertising messages. Broadcasters instinctively preferred reticence in sales announcements. Radio's broad purpose was to entertain, to inform, and to enhance the listeners' perceptions of the world of music and literature and talk and sport as well as of depression and war. Local broadcast companies and national networks set aside portions of their schedules for experimental efforts precisely because they were not expected to attract massive audiences sought by advertisers. Those "sustaining" shows without commercial sponsorship, underwritten by the radio companies, became the workshops for inventive minds such as Norman Corwin and Orson Welles.

Just after the Second World War, the FCC in 1946 distributed its *Public Service Responsibility of Broadcast Licensees.* That booklet (dubbed the "Blue Book" for the color of its cover) urged some balance between advertising-supported and commercial-free sustaining programs in broadcast schedules, precisely to permit socially and culturally valued programs free of pressures to reach absolutely mass audiences dear to sponsors.

In such a context Mr. Corwin and his colleagues at CBS, along with other creative spirits at networks and at local stations in communities across the nation, could test the young medium and stretch it—and thereby stretch the perceptions and imagination of selective audiences—with creative experiences in sound. The power of the written word crafted in poetic cadences, articulated by the living human voice, accompanied by live musicians and manually created sound effects combined to conjure up Prospero's entrancing magic at the service of a mass medium.

Today, alas, not only most broadcasters but even the government regulator themselves have abandoned any pretense at contributing to the public weal in terms of social, cultural values. In effect, they have forsaken the original legislators' insight (in 1927 and 1934) into the civilizing role of media, in favor of a strictly mercantile, commerce-oriented role. The buzzwords are "marketplace" and "marketplace forces."

The tradition is not without respectable antecedents. Jefferson and Holmes looked to a free, pluralistic society's "marketplace of ideas" instead of government ukase as the catalyst for democratic interaction and decision-making. But the tradition has eroded. From that ideological marketplace, emphasis in the 1980s has swung to strictly economic reality: the forces of commerce in a literal marketplace of buyers and sellers of goods and services. Broadcast media have come to be seen as pragmatic instruments serving those marketing forces of manufacturers who advertise.

Broadcasters' objectives are no longer primarily to create sensitive and enlightening forms of *communication* (which Professor George Gordon defines as the process of transacting human meaning). Instead, dominant and even sole objectives are to reach massive audiences with demographic characteristics sought and highly paid for by advertisers. Rather than creating programs to serve the public, broadcasters craft programs that will serve up the public to clients. The business of radio and television has as its product the audience which it sells to clients in carloads of a thousand (the unit measure being CPM, or cost-per-thousand), with programs merely the bait to attract them. Or more precisely, as broadcast manager Dan O'Brien notes, broadcasters are really in the business of "attention rental." They schedule shows that catch the listening or viewing public's attention; then they attempt to hold that attention by means of the program so the audience will be exposed to intermittent commercial messages. At the program's end, the broadcaster goes his way and the audience members go their way. In the meantime, their attention has been made available to the commercial blandishments of the highest-bidding advertiser, who pays for the entire process.

This is a far cry from the halcyon days of early radio when the creative artist and the discriminating audience were paramount, at least for substantial, regularly scheduled sustaining program series.

If the 1930s and 1940s were years of creative development in radio, the 1950s and 1960s saw broadcasters at least held to some accountability to American society by the federal regulatory agency, whose chairman during the John Kennedy administration castigated them for a "vast wasteland" of programming. The social upheavals that shook the domestic and international scene in that latter decade spawned increased attention to news and socially relevant drama and even comedy forms in television. Those forms fortuitously attracted audiences and thus advertisers and thus profits. By the late 1970s some of those forms were self-imitative and pandered with less substantive content and format to ensure popularity and profitability. By the permissive 1980s, members of Congress were following the lead of broadcast executives and FCC officials who lobbied for surcease from governmental oversight of radio and television.

Perhaps part of the historical problem lay in bureaucracy's attempting to impose salvation upon the majority of nonbelievers in the broadcasting industry. The FCC's 1960 statement on programming clearly noted broadcasters' obligation of service to their communities: "The principal ingredient of such obligation consists of a diligent, positive and continuing effort by the licensee to discover and fulfill the tastes, needs and desires of his service area. If he has accomplished this he has met his public responsibility." That mandate emphasized the public who received broadcasts, not the investor or owner of broadcast properties nor the advertisers. But it did lead to a plethora of forms, procedures, mechanical compliance, and sometimes no very creative local or live or otherwise dynamic programming. So subsequent FCC chairmen and the many supporters of this movement to disengage broadcasting from government bureaucracy did have some valid reasons for what they proposed. Technicalities of paperwork and compliance with distantly mandated federal guidelines at times smothered true responsiveness to their local communities by acquiescing broadcaster determined to retain their lucrative licenses. Vexing complications in applying regulations, such as the "fairness doctrine" about topics of public controversy, and "equal opportunities" (or "equal time") for candidates for public office, and other requirements to achieve technically clean stewardship, inhibite as well as advanced open and free discourse through radio and television.

Members of the Senate and House of Representatives in the 1980s strove unfetter electronic media by proposing major amendments to the Communications Act of 1934; some sought to dismantle that legislation and proposed complete rewriting of it or substitution of wholly new laws granting broadcast media parity to print media under the First Amendment. FCC chairmen of both major parties successively endeavored to loosen the ties that bound broadcasters to the "national nanny of the regulatory agency.

The clearest expression of this radical shift in philosophy and priorities about broadcasting in American society was candidly laid out by FCC chairman Mark Fowler during the first term of the Reagan administration. In 1982 he articulately outlined the cas for abandoning the traditional "public interest" standard for those holding federally granted licenses to broadcast. He straightforwardly advanced the more restrained efforts of his predecessors in the FCC chair, Republican Richard Wiley and Democrat Charles Ferris. On strictly legal and technical grounds (the proper arena for public policy), he cited the rationale of spectrum scarcity and the basic fiduciary principle (mandate by the Communications Act of 1934 "to serve the public interest, convenience, and necessity") as faulty and obsolete premises for contemporary governmental oversight of the airwaves—considered through all previous decades as a national resource of the American public. The intangible "ether" or "airwaves" were deemed no longer comparable to the nation's navigable waterways, to be protected analogously for the good of all citizens; instead they were properties of commerce to be operated by owners almost exclusively as instruments of profit-making.

Professor Dallas Smythe lamented that the FCC's formal statements and actions in the late 1970s and early 1980s would lead to the result "that the public which owns the radio frequencies will be deprived of protection of its rights to receive radio service necessary for its educational, social, cultural, and political welfare—rights won in struggles in the Congress, the regulatory agency, and the courts over more than half a century."

Chairman Fowler confirmed those worst fears because what had once been the major motivating factor for broadcasters was now to become the sole motivating criterion: "Once the Commission concludes that the best service for the public lies with a market system where licensees can air programs designed to attract the largest audiences for advertisers or the largest subscriber base, it can refrain from reviewing programming and other licensee decisions." That goes far beyond normal First Amendment concerns about regulating content, to the vast agenda of all "other licensee decisions"!

The concept of "marketplace" was acknowledged by the FCC's chairman as possibly broader than merely mercantile; he referred to "the marketplace, speaking through advertisers, critics, and self-selection by viewers." Again, "perceived listener demand" is the criterion for program scheduling, and "satisfaction of listener interests" will result in "programming that best serves the people."

But this leaves in limbo anything beyond merely reacting to polls and ratings services that show what kinds of programs audiences spend most time with. It leaves unanswered the nagging question about alternate kinds of programming not now on the schedules. How does one find out, with merely commerce and profits as the touchstone for "service," what audiences might want in addition to or instead of the limited range of standardized fare? As the late Franklin Dunham, who served at NBC and the U.S. Office of Education, was fond of recommending: "Give the public what it wants most of the time, and a little of what it would want if it only knew about it." Instead, broadcasters are free to give the public not what it may truly want and even need, but simply more of what it already consumes on the shaky inference that this is all that it wants. The "public interest" is more than what merely "interests the public" from day to day. Creative leadership is different from imitative followership because it knows that good taste comes from tasting good things, from exposure to excellence—which must have opportunity for expression whether or not massive crowds initially recognize and support such.

The FCC chairman's move in the 1980s to abdicate concern for other than factors of profitable commerce is a chilling regression from the early years when Norman Corwin and his network colleagues could tantilize and inspire not inconsequential segments of the national population through a medium that nurtured rather than neutered creativity.

The medium (part industry, part art), supported and prompted by the regulatory FCC, offered an environment for innovative risk-taking in radio. Radio fostered the emergence of self-expression for an entire nation. This was the townsquare open to poetry, music, sound, and thought—through radio. It was an electronic meeting place of a nation's people. Not merely a marketplace. And it commissioned this reflection on the nation's forging of peace, putting itself at the service of Mr. Corwin—whom the *Los Angeles Times* has referred to as probably the only authentic genius in radio. (Perhaps the closest we have come since then to a medium's serving as a means of national self-reflection without thought of commerce was during the solemn tragedy of the Kennedy assassination weekend in 1963. A distant second manifestation might have been the tortuously extended coverage of self-doubt and judgment during the Vietnam years.)

In those instances radio and television constituted the national townsquare, not the cluttered marketplace. And it might be relevant to note that the Greek marketplace *(ἀγορα)* which was the venue for Socrates' explorations into concepts and reasoning was not wholly open to creative interchange. When that philosopher's musings upset the accepted and common status quo, "marketplace forces" of his own day led to hemlock and death.

The direction given to the FCC in the 1980s by its chairman shifted the original concept from a "marketplace of ideas" among enlightened people engaged in robust discourse to a pragmatic "marketplace of competitive commerce" for private gain. Repeated reference to the people as "consumers" rather than as "public" or "audience" reflects stress on the media as vehicles for efficient advertising, not as conduits for civilization. Chairman Fowler made his intent clear: "Our thesis is that the perception of broadcasters as community trustees should be replaced by a view of broadcasters as marketplace participants." He did grant that communication policy ought be "directed toward maximizing the services the public desires," but "the Commission should rely on the broadcasters' ability to determine the wants of their audiences through the normal mechanisms of the marketplace" as commercial competitors. He noted that major problems arise in broadcast media with the trusteeship model of the past because the broadcasters' responsibility "officially runs to the viewing public as defined by the Commission, not to shareholders, sponsors, or even the users of the sponsors' products or services who indirectly finance the stations." What could be clearer? "Marketplace" was not to refer exclusively to financial investments and to movement of goods and services, with programming merely the enticing bait by which to attract mass numbers of potential consumers. Worse, the listening and viewing public was no longer defined as the community of people with their diverse interests and needs but instead limited to revenue-generating consumers of products who were the concern of shareholders and advertisers.

All of which has little to do with creative broadcasting represented by the innovators and creators of Mr. Corwin's era.

The FCC's chairman looked to the 1980s and beyond as a time when individual broadcasters will feel unfettered of technical regulatory demands and will thus be free to respond to their own perception of what people in their communities really want. Yet even an industry-oriented trade magazine, *Broadcast/Management Engineering,* was becoming uneasy when it editorialized in August of 1984 about the deregulatory movement:

> ...If U.S. broadcasters were like those in other countries, used to the responsibility of providing the populace with a varied diet of entertainment, news, public affairs, and the occasional commercial, such an action would be a signal of the government's confidence in its broadcast organizations. But this is not the case here. Broadcasting has grown up with the singular purpose of making a profit, and the government has seen its role as insuring the public interest. It has been a healthy relationship, one born in the best traditions of American democracy....
>
> Jean-Jacques Rousseau observed that man (like broadcasting) was born free, and everywhere he is in chains (governmental regulation). Rousseau advocated setting man free by providing him with the tools of reason. But does suddenly removing the chains of regulation from an industry that has never known anything else, and expecting it to restrain itself when it has never needed to do anything but resist government rulemaking towards the end of making a profit, reflect a sensible approach to human nature?

But these considerations did not concern the FCC official. He unmistakably concluded his treatise by stating: "commercial broadcasters would be absolutely free to pursue commercial objectives without lingering trusteeship obligations." There you have it. The head of the federal agency established to regulate broadcasting abjured any further role in supporting responsible and responsive commercial programming, except as wholly responsive to advertisers' strategic purposes.

Mr. Fowler tipped his hand when he abruptly linked mass media and social and cultural consciousness by putting that whole matter at the doorstep of non-commercial, public broadcasting. The mission and mandate formerly directed to the powerful broadcast corporations (whose revenue was derived from federally licensed stations' advertising) were now to be redirected to the scattered, partly federally funded public radio and television stations. So Chairman Fowler would say that innovative, creative, civilizing programming can still survive despite the FCC's capitulation to commercialism, but only on the frequencies reserved for non-commercial programming—thus relieving commercial companies from any further concern for such small-audience efforts. Pay cable networks and other commercial- and profit-oriented broadcasters, he noted, "are likely to skim the most popular cultural programs, leaving little support for emerging but less marketable talent." Children, minorities, the elderly, creative artists, and other individuals wishing access as well as a diversity of alternative fare can all be served nicely, in Fowler's view, by the public outlets. He chose not to mention that in

a typical U.S. community there is only one non-commercial television station (usually UHF) and perhaps one or two low-powered FM public stations—as compared with literally dozens of commercial radio stations and a half dozen television stations. Some access! Some creative opportunity! Some source of diverse, alternative programming!

Former Governor of Florida LeRoy Collins once noted during his short tenure as president of the National Association of Broadcasters (which trade organization swiftly dumped him soon after these remarks): "Broadcasting to serve the public interest must have a soul and a conscience, a burning desire to excel, as well as to sell; the urge to build the character, citizenship and intellectual stature of people, as well as to expand the gross national product." That sounds more like the spirit animating a Norman Corwin and some of the early broadcast executives who, while often hyphenates out of other businesses and entertainment fields, had instinctive respect for the growing medium of radio as a medium of communication more than one of commerce.

That's why we refer to them as "the good old days!"

And the pendulum does swing both ways. Many broadcasters anticipate—some with dread, others with hope—that future administrators and lawmakers will reflect sentiment and judgment by the public at large and by responsible, caring people in the media.

In the meantime, one might be cheered by reading Norman Corwin's own assessment of the evolving mass media, which he wrote for the concluding program in CBS' week-long, prime-time celebration of its fiftieth anniversary. What some perceive as a hideous giant may still be a magnificent adolescent—with or without government's regulatory restraints. Despite past lapses, and noting the cornucopia of broadcast developments in the tumultuous twentieth century, there is yet "more to come."

This offers lingering hope to creative souls who look to American broadcasting as symbol-producing and culture-maintaining media contributing to social structures, not as merely marketing tools for mass consumerism. Dr. Theodore Gill (Dean and Provost of John Jay College of Criminal Justice in New York) encouraged those engaged in children's television to persist with devoted energy. His words can encourage thoughtful broadcasters, media artists, and discriminating audiences alike:

> What I am asking for is your own poetry, your pictures, your hunches, your visions, your obsessions, your prime-time scratching of your most personal itches—that's what we need. The powers that be will work their nervous ways on your materials, and maybe necessarily so, but start high anyway, personally, excitedly, in the deeps of your mysterious individuality.

It sounds as if the contagious spirit of Norman Corwin is still loose in the land, the federal deregulatory agency's preoccupation with the profits of doom notwithstanding.

Words

ROBERT E. LEE

Jenny is mad at me. She cannot understand why I cannot understand her.

In some measure, of course, I can. A grandfather is not a total idiot. And it is possible, even in my tattered state of grace, to grasp *some* of the pronouncements of a young lady who has just completed her first circuit of the Sun. As I listen to her, I have that same sense of uneasiness that I've felt recently in conferences with confreres from China or from the U.S.S.R.: we communicate with our eyes and faces, with intonations and gestures. From time to time, we pick up a few sounds that have a shared meaning. I've always suspected that my Soviet and Chinese friends were more deft at this language game than I. As for Jenny, there's no doubt about it: she absorbs from me far more than my wisdom-stiff perception draws from her.

Though Jenny is articulate, her sounds are only rarely particulate. Whole paragraphs of the incomprehensible pour forth with an expectation that I will get the gist of it. But there is no handy earpiece, no translator hidden in a booth somewhere to sort out the comprehensible denominators of communication. As far as Jenny is concerned, I have flunked my entrance examination for admission to her world.

Sometimes I try to respond in kind to the cornucopiae of noises from her one-year-old larynx. I erupt into a pseudo-rational gibberish, in an effort to counterfeit hers.

For an instant, her eyes light up. She seems to be saying: "At last! A little *sense* out of this guy!" But then her glance goes askance: she knows I'm faking.

Inwardly, she sighs. For Jenny is forgiving and wise. This little girl knows that eventually she will have to adjust the parameters of *her* speech-field to accommodate the more orderly syntax of mine.

I underwent an acute attack of language at an impressionable age. By the mere accident of turning the knob on my car radio, I was infected by exposure to Norman Corwin. Fortunately, I have never recovered. Corwin is clearly a carrier of "word-fever." His elevating fervor can precipitate epidemics of epic proportions. (My own temperature has never come down!)

From Norman I learned to frame questions that can't really be answered; for questions are always more interesting than answers, and far less final.

Is speech gestalt? The speed-reading people would like us to think so. They urge us to gobble whole paragraphs and pages by the undifferentiated mouthful. I suspect that Jenny, too, would like to think that each sentence is a lungful long. Is an idea a sudden swash of meaning?—a splash of sound across the al fresco wall of air?

Can we learn anything from the embryology of language? I don't hold that you have to tear the wings off a butterfly to appreciate its beauty. But don't we miss some of the joy of using language if we ignore its components?

Communicating is more complex than arranging a mosaic of words. Each word is a mosaic of letters. I marvel at my typewriter keyboard. A piano has 88 keys. A typewriter has half that number—and about half of those are mere frills and arithmetic symbols. Yet the whole towering literature of Western Man has been built from these few basic blocks—everything from the Holy Bible to next month's issue of Playboy.

The alphabet is a greater invention than the wheel. Simple? Perhaps. Yet the ingenious men of the Orient never stumbled on it. Half of civilization still uses complex picture-writing and ideograms instead of this simple typewriter keyboard. And in Eastern countries, this drew a sharp line between those who could absorb wisdom from markings scratched on paper (or vellum or moist clay) and those who couldn't. Result? A sharply delineated literary elite.

But in the West, more and more words were crowding into the minds of more and more people—from Plato to Jerome to Jefferson. Democracy soars on the wings of the A-B-C's. Was it the lack of an alphabet which kept the masses of the East in fealty to Shoguns and Manchu Emperors until recent times?

Where was the alphabet invented? Who dreamed up the astonishing notion that men could make paper talk? I don't particularly trust Pliny the Elder. (He is that haphazard historian who had the bad judgment to be visiting friends in Herculaneum when Vesuvius blew her top.) Pliny says the sailors of Phoenicia were the first men to concoct a phonetic alphabet.

It's appealing, isn't it, to imagine some Pre-Punic Ancient Mariner, standing watch before the mast at the sunrise of the race. Perhaps he has just been to Egypt, where he was baffled by the hieroglyphics on an obelisk. Or maybe he has puzzled over some baked-clay tablets from Babylon, or the crude picture-writing of even more primitive peoples.

Then, suddenly, the *idea*!—clear as the morning-star over the Aegean. Why not make a separate mark for each sound a man speaks? "A" for the open vowel across the flattened tongue, "B" for a burst of breath between the lips—and so on. From one simple package of symbols, speech could become permanent. Men long dead could talk to us from markings on a page of papyrus or vellum. Oral tradition could be congealed—rescued from the inaccuracies of repetition, the erosion of memory. The wisdom (and foolishness) of the race could be made to last forever.

Did it happen that way? In our hankering for heroes, we like to think that one man, one mind is responsible for landmark achievements. But creation, in its larger scale, tends to be collective, collaborative. I doubt if the mosaics with which we write were delivered in such a Mosaic flash. Isn't it more likely that putting man's voice on paper (or its ancient equivalent) was not a solo but a choral accomplishment? And it may have spread over generations, even centuries. From the shabby scraps of writing which they left us, the inventors of the Great Mother Alphabet didn't seem to know what to do with these precious blocks they gave us to play with. But they gave the human race a "sound track": The rolling cadences of Hebrew, the terse economy of Greek, the melody of the Romance languages, the plosive convolutions of German, and our own polyglot hodge-podge of English—all are rooted in the same double baker's-dozen of signs!

What happens when we start to put them together? These letters and symbols we play with are like the gritty heads of comets—miniscule in mass, but awesome in their luminescence. Why does a comet have a fiery tail? As it nears the sun, it is responding to the impact of the solar wind. In the outer reaches of its orbit, a comet is a cold, sluggish conglomerate of interplanetary gravel.

Then it plunges toward the light, testing its speed against the pull of the star which locks it in a long ellipse. The stony nucleus stirs to life, whipped around the sun by the lash of gravity.

Can *words* be comets? Do they carry bright clouds of context, signaling to us with a glow of multiple meanings? What radiant ideas may splay out from the near-weightless nucleus of syllables!

My own first professional interest (as you may have guessed) is astronomy. Norman Corwin is a gemologist. He collects and admires the exceptional stones which make our earth-space more interesting (just as stars enhance the void of space beyond this blue planet). And each of Norman's gems is a universe in itself. It emits its own unique glow. The shades of its trans-lingual meaning differ each time the ambient light changes. Herein lies the perpetual astonishment of suns, precious stones, and words. They defy definition. Catalogues and dictionaries notwithstanding, stars, words, and gems are constantly aflame, turning themselves into what they never were, burning themselves into beacons that we never imagined they could be.

What discoveries are stored up for a one-year-old! Jenny is learning the ecstasy of closeness and distance. She can hold sand in her hand, and the stars are only slightly beyond her fingertips.

Now the land-birds are circling above her head. She has sighted the terra nova of words. Soon, soon Jenny's keel will scrape the beach of speech. She is a sailor far more fortunate than the old Phoenician:

Corwin is waiting for her!

12 The Radio Generation

Leonard Leader

The radio box with its talk and music was unknown before KDKA told us in 1920 that the Republican Warren Harding had beaten the Democrat James Cox for president of our country. Radio's entrance into our homes was a complete entertainment invasion. It was new and heard in every corner. I can recall my older cousin, Albert, in New York (1922) fine-tuning his crackling crystal set and announcing with triumph one morning that he had stayed up to A.M. hours and gotten Florida. There were some who claimed to have heard Denver, Colorado, from the far West.

Confess I must, that in the twenties we had no radio; we listened to our neighbor's or relative's set. Were we that poor or did poppa think that radio was a passing fad? The truth is, he was never even comfortable with the telephone and shouted into it, much louder if it was a long distance call. When he did listen, he leaned towards the radio, sure to catch every word of the news bulletin.

I can hear the program *The Happiness Boys,* a duo, singing in high voices and always ending with a commercial jingle pushing Interwoven Socks. There was a mixed-up day in Brooklyn's Madison High School's Annex 216, with classes cancelled so that we could assemble in the cold barn of an auditorium with a stage bare of all but a chair on which sat a small static-filled radio trying to give us the bands and sounds of Herbert Hoover's inauguration. It was March 4, 1929, not radio's finest hour, but it was wonderful not to have the regular classes that day.

Radio also brought us to our school auditorium on Fridays to listen to conductor Dr. Walter Damrosch with his avuncular talk about musical instruments and renditions of the classics. "This my children is the sound of a French Horn; this is how you will recognize Schubert's *Unfinished Symphony*. . . ." At times there were dreaded written music recognition tests.

Soap operas first foamed on radio. Vast audiences listened for decades to the straight and simple dramas of *Myrt and Marge*, two ladies who spent much time on the telephone; *Just Plain Bill* with his earthy advice and wisdom; *Helen Trent* long entwined with love and its problems; and wasn't there an orphan girl from the West who followed her love to the East? Did they last only 15 minutes? The operas were there every day, and one dramatizing the *Bible* was very popular. The Friday chapters ended with serious crises, big enough to worry you over the weekend and eager for the Monday slice.

Long before the wars of the stars there was *Buck Rogers and the Twenty First Century*, and space guns and space helmets. Did you know that *Spider Man* almost daily climbed up straight walls in his role of crime fighter? (Weren't those the days when crime and even sex were simpler?)

Every Saturday *Let's Pretend* dramatized favorite fairy tales, and no fairy flew more gracefully and poetically than the ones on radio. We had read *Cinderella, Hansel and Gretel, Jack and the Beanstalk*, and on Saturdays we heard them. What beautiful voices; who can forget the charm of *Beauty and the Beast* or the *Sleeping Beauty*? And how many of those tales ended with the advice to ask mother for "the breakfast food of champions"?

Sunday night was reserved for Eddie Cantor. Songs and guests, and always the bouncing jubilant Cantor "who loved to spend this hour with you," and told all that "tomatoes were cheaper, potatoes were cheaper, and now was the time to fall in love."

What an amplifier the radio was for comedians. National fame came to Fred Allen and his *Allen's Alley* where he went door to door quizzing characters such as the beknighted Southern Senator Claghorn, Mrs. Nussbaum, Titus Moody, and other offbeat souls each with whimsies of their own. There were regular comedy programs devoted to Molly Goldberg who held forth over the rear yard clothesline; sections of variety shows which propelled George Jessel, Joe Penner (everyone knew his line—"wanna buy a duck?") and the immortal Groucho Marx, and the one-liner Henny Youngman, a radio hit on Kate Smith's variety hour. (She was completely identified with the song "When the Moon Comes Over the Mountain.")

And there were the nights we went four blocks to Uncle Alex's and Aunt Polly's house to hear *The Shadow,* a mystery. We listened with all the lights out to feed the imagination, while our impish older cousin, Abele, added scary noises of his own.

My wife Rita recalls an upsetting night when one touched the radio dial to make it louder or clearer and accidentally lost the station and the mystery in a tense moment. What cries beset one. Never again would one touch the sacred box while in operation in company!

Or hot, Brooklyn summer nights, we stood on the sidewalk in front of a neighbor's porch where a kindly radio owner turned his set up so that we might hear the heavyweight fights—Dempsey, Tunney, Schmeling, and the great Joe Louis. "A right to the jaw, a left to the jaw...." Only with television did Rita realize that there was a process of hurting, bleeding, and the closing of swollen eyes. On radio there was the antiseptic count of "9, 10, and he's out." The glamour was radio's; on television it became gore.

In the early 1930s, we bought a radio—a large console type, a ponderous piece of furniture some three feet high with a record player within that never worked well. The coming of the great radio into our house was a concession to the news that the Metropolitan Opera Company would broadcast the opera every Saturday. The folks thought it was culturally acceptable now to allow a radio into the house. Lily Pons in *Lakmé, Lucia di Lammermoor,* Lauritz Melchoir, Rosa Ponselle, Kirsten Flagstad and *Rigoletto* and, and.... And always the voice of Milton Cross telling us the stories and the biographies of the great singers and composers.

In those pioneer days the staccato voice of H.V. Kaltenborn brought news from many fronts; we became life long addicts of the smooth voice of Lowell Thomas who always ended with "so long until tomorrow."

A boarder in momma's house listened daily to a baseball game described by an announcer who recreated the action against the background of the informative clack of the telegrapher's key. The man at the radio station saw no game, he only saw the tape strips, but his voice and excitement made us see the full game. Millions of sportslovers were wed to their radios in pursuit of the games and the scores. (Still goes on.) Sportscaster Graham McNamee was a national idol.

The London fog filtered into our living rooms as the warm and inquiring voices of Sherlock Holmes and Dr. Watson gave us a weekly tale of creaking hinges, winds whipping over the moors, the shuffling of feet, dragging objects, and vicious growls of hounds. The commercial sponsors still stick in my mind—G. Washington Coffee, tablets which became coffee as the steaming water dissolved them in your cup. Did you smell the coffee as you heard the stirring spoon? We never bought the product; poppa said it cost too much.

Great audiences came to *Amos and Andy,* a white rascist view of blacks; their successful advertiser was Pepsodent, but my parents would not buy the dentrifice and never let us listen to the program.

Early on, we were indoctrinated with the need of advertising on the radio, but somehow the messages did not come as often, as blatantly and interruptive as they seem to come on television. We did know that Lee DeForest, father of radio, had complained about radio's commercialization crying out "what have you done with my child...you have cut time into tiny parcels called spots (more rightly 'stains')...the occasionally fine program is periodically smeared with imprudent insistence to buy or try...yet I am still proud of my child."

Radio voices of the leaders and the misleaders of the world sounded loudly in our living rooms in that quarter of a century from KDKA to Norman Corwin's *On a Note of Triumph* saying the great war was won. Some tones were smooth and soft; some were strident and savage. Didn't our radio generation produce FDR, a radio President and presence who chatted with us at the fireside, and made us feel he was compassionate and cared?

I recall the homespun Southern voice of Huey Long one evening inviting us to call in our neighbors to come and hear him. He was populist enough to know that not everyone had a radio. Or his spiritual ally, the more sophisticated Father Charles Coughlin of Royal Oaks, Michigan, who every Sunday morning reached millions beyond his parish with pro-silver and anti-semitism as his messages. On that radio base, he built a national organization and a weekly paper sold by an army of supporters who walked the streets, held corner open-air meetings offering simplistic and crude answers to a nation convulsed in a mighty depression.

From Europe, came the growling gutteral voice screaming with emotion and hate announcing that today he ruled Germany and "tomorrow the world." Conquests were trumpeted and the radio filled us with days of terror from Vienna, Munich, Prague, Dunkerque, the road to Moscow. Finally on December 7, 1944 the popular Sunday afternoon radio broadcast of the New York Philharmonic was interrupted with the chilling news that Japanese bombs were dropping on a place called Pearl Harbor. In the days that followed, the nation reacted to the "day in infamy" heard on the radio. The fireside chats became the voice of a world on fire as we marched to war.

Bombed London brought us the voice of Edward R. Murrow daily. Bob Hope came into our barracks from some military base every Tuesday night and we all laughed at his one liners as we lay in our bunks—even the soldier with the endless guitar rendition of "You Are My Sunshine" took time off.

One barracks morning, June 6, 1944, to be exact, we started the day not with the radio sending us South Carolina hill music, but the voice of FDR with a prayer and an announcement that we were landing in Normandy for the final conflict with Hitler. Radio brought the sound of exploding shells and we did not seem to miss the sights, for many soldiers remember combat as mostly frightening sound.

We followed the war through Gabriel Heatter who was so upbeat in his radio reports that we named him "old satchel bag" for it seemed that we would soon pack our bags and go home. He dramatized in orotound fashion the dilemmas of Hitler as defeats piled up. "Old Hitler is eating the rug he is pacing tonight" is a mixed image I recall.

Radio was also a tool of the enemy. Soldiers were given defeatist messages from Lord Haw Haw in Berlin and Tokyo Rose who tried vocal seduction. Never was radio such a failure.

One late night, the German radio told us that our President was dead. I debunked it as Nazi propaganda until our radio told us "he died at Warm Springs, Georgia...Harry Truman was just sworn in...."

We bear the title "Radio Generation" honorably. It followed us for a quarter of a century in all the intricacies of our lives. What factory did not have an umbrella of radio music to soothe assemblers of monotonous parts; workers listening to Martin Block's *Make Believe Ballroom* with the top song hits.

On Saturday night, young dancers everywhere in ballrooms, house parties, cellar clubs swayed to Lucky Strike's *Hit Parade,* featuring Ben Bernie, Benny Goodman, Glenn Miller, Gene Krupa, and many more of the great bands. Can we forget that "the music goes round and round," and that "baby and me and Molly makes three in my blue heaven," and the laments of war that "they're either too young or too old," and it was preferable to have "a paper doll I could call my own," or the soldier's admonition that she not "sit under the apple tree with anybody else but me," and the realization that radio, like love and life had "that old black magic in its spell."

Magic and radio did have a spell deepened by those unknown sound men who made running water, the crack of axes against trees, the clopping hooves of the *Lone Ranger* setting off into the hills. Their devices captured the rain and the wind, the boom of the gun, and the twang of the arrow. One could almost hear the sun setting on the far horizon.

The glory of radio was its partnership with your mind and limitless imagination. Within your head you wove a mental tapestry richer in color and texture than any picture tube could equal. On Fridays, as a high school senior I would run home from school to catch classical British plays rebroadcast from London. What pageants paraded in our being fed by the flow of language from the land that gave us William Shakespeare, John Milton, and George Bernard Shaw.

Out of the many radio offerings came many great moments. In the Valhalla at the peak stand the dramas of Norman Corwin with his melodic rhythms—great epics of poetic sound. How often did my wife and I sit on a living room sofa in our courting days (does anyone know what that was?) to listen to the plays of Corwin and Arch Oboler. We can still feel and hear the vibration of the hospital bed spring from the dramatization of Dalton Trumbo's stark *Johnny Got His Gun.*

For our radio generation, the memories are full. The offerings were mixed, but all in all, to steal a Corwin phrase, there were many "sweet influences."

13 The Celebrator

Earl Robinson

There is a peculiar importance to the timing. As I sit down to think on Norman Corwin, what he means and what he has meant, the historic July, 1984 Democratic Convention is in full swing in San Francisco. This gathering is choosing its standard bearer and an accepted part of this choosing is a charismatic black man and the consuming presence of a woman uniting sisters with brothers, equal for the first time in American politics.

As the theme of peace emerges strongly, the dream of a non-nuclear weapons world wholly, firmly on the agenda, my mind goes back to the summer of 1945 in San Francisco. Norman Corwin and I, Lud Gluskin, and others were helping CBS salute the budding United Nations on CBS Radio. Two songs of mine with the great E.Y. (Yippur) Harburg, "Same Boat Brother" and "Ain't You Comin' to the Meetin'" were being performed by Alfred Drake at this early-on vision of Peace, Equality, and Brotherhood. In the control room, firmly in charge as he always was, Norman sat and made the whole thing go, properly. Norman was later to widen this vision with his apocalyptic *On a Note of Triumph,* spelling out in some detail the kind of world available to us, if we wanted it enough and were willing to learn some lessons. My part in *Note* was smaller. I helped Pete Seeger and the Almanac Singers sing "Round and Round Hitler's Grave."

I remember that most pregnant radio occasion in '45 for two bits of dialogue in the song "Ain't Ya Comin' to the Meetin'," that I got to say. One, "Blondes, Brunettes and Clarinets." The other, dedicated to the main architect of the U.N., Franklin Delano Roosevelt, who had passed on just a month before. Replying to the line "Too bad Franklin D. couldn't make it" the answer was "He'll *be there,*" a theme I have come to accept as a commonplace truth—that there is no death, just "change of place" as Chief Seattle put it.

That was the first and last time those two songs were sung on the air. I see the present-day Democrats as being in a good position, finally, to program them. Especially "Same Boat Brother" with its refrain "If you shake one end you're gonna rock the other!" This has gone on like a folk song. Ledbelly picked it up and sang it for a time, but it has not yet been on radio or TV.

Another important radio program happened the year before in October of 1944. Also, with obvious connections to San Francisco '84. Roosevelt was running for an unprecedented 4th term and this was a Demo "Commercial" on CBS Radio, directed by Corwin. Judy Garland sang a song of Yip's and mine, "Gotta Get Out and Vote," while Norman had the pleasant job of routining a long line of actresses and actors who were standing and waiting to state their names for Roosevelt again. "Linda Darnell," "Joe Cotton for the old Man," and so on. Dropping names here, Groucho Marx, Danny Kaye, James Cagney, and a fourth I can't remember, sang in a quartet a song about the "Good Old Days." Yip wrote a number for Jimmy Durante, where he changed all my music...a riot of a song "19thoity two I was in business for meself, sellin' apples! And that man in duh White House regimented me into a good job!"

So, I knew Norman as essentially a celebrator. (It probably takes one to know one.) Given the heaviest scene, the most earnest of situations, he would find a way of lightening—while retaining all the original juices. Being an original himself, he came with understanding and respect for the different, the special. Our first experience together was in the fall of 1939, New York City. I came to him asking for advice on a dramatic cantata of mine called "Ballad of Uncle Sam." This piece was the finale of a Musical Revue, one of the Federal Theatre WPA hits, "Sing for

Your Supper." Everything this theatrical creature of the depression produced was a hit including "The Living Newspaper," "A Black Voodoo Macbeth," etc. This was the place where Orson Welles and John Houseman got their start. In this quite exciting showcase, "Sing for Your Supper" had more trouble than most. Fourteen months in rehearsal, under special attack from the Republicans and Southern Democrats in Congress, it closed after just a five-week run and was the beginning of the end of the whole project. WPA had finally succumbed, not just to the virulence of the reactionaries' attack, but to an inexorable economic upswing occasioned by a war and a war economy on the horizon.

So back (forward) to Norman Corwin who was an important creative force on CBS Radio during this whole period. In addition to his own original, exciting writing-producing, he had just taken on the job of directing a new CBS Sustainer Special, *Pursuit of Happiness.*

I sang for him John Latouche's and my "Ballad of Uncle Sam," and he immediately saw the possibility of programming it on *Pursuit of Happiness.* He took me up to the CBS Brass where I presented it again at the piano. And Bill Lewis, a vice president, I believe, opened up a whole new history for the piece with his remark "Wouldn't Robeson knock the hell out of this!" Out of his mouth into God's ears. I learned later that CBS had approached Big Paul to be on the *Pursuit of Happiness* but decided his price was too high. (I think Robeson's agent was asking a thousand dollars, a lot of money for a sustainer at that time.) Anyway, after hearing the Ballad, they decided to hire him.

The result is history. I met Big Paul. We rehearsed for a week in almost complete harmony. I have never had such a totally cooperative relationship. He was determined to sing-talk the piece the way I wanted it. Only one disagreement, about pitch. He kept insisting on moving it *down* into what I regarded as a subterranean basso range. I lost that argument when he told me the Soviets transposed *Boris Godounow* entirely into his range. "Seems lik you might be able to do the same for me, huh?"

Norman's contribution, besides presenting, directing Mark Warnow's orchesra, Lyn Murray's chorus, and Robeson with impeccable excitement was to rename the piece. He simply announced it was to be "Ballad for Americans." Nobody, including me, saw any reason to argue.

Anyway it all added up in November of 1939. The teamwork which as a characteristic of Corwin gelled into a presentation that had a studio audience on their feet applauding for five minutes afte the climactic "America." CBS switchboards were jammed in New York and Hollywood for two hours after the program; more than 500 letters came in the next few days. The show had to be repeated on New Year's Day. Other subsequent events included the publication and recording of "Ballad" and its sale to MGM for a picture. And Robeson kept singing it.

An interesting conflict occurred in July of 1940. The Lewison Stadium wa programming "Ballad for Americans" the same night the Republican Party had scheduled the piece for their Presidential (Wilkie) Convention. Big Paul evidently had little trouble choos ing to sing it at Lewison Stadium. But John Latouche and I wer some confused. Interviewed by the New Yorker on this awkward contretemps, "We wrote the 'Ballad' for everybody, not only Republicans," said Mr. Latouche. "Especially not only ...Republicans," said Mr. Robeson.

This dramatic cantata, which Norman Corwin had produced so professionally, was to move—first with Robeson, later on its own, in directions Democratic. I note in passing some of these. High schools, colleges, community choruses wanted to sing it, and the complete Democrat Robeson never missed a chance to do i with them, often with just a piano in place of the symphonic version. Some of the most moving "Ballad" productions have since been done with grade school children here in the United States.

My relationship with Corwin, the Norman, was, I am realising, almost entirely professional. However, we started out in a pre-professional—he in Hollywood, I in New York—manner after the "Ballad" excitement when he agreed to work long distance on Carl Sandburg's *The People, Yes.* Both of us, separately, had established pretty good relations with that fine and sensitive poet. Norman had already dramatized *The People, Yes* in his radio programs, developing satiric elements that Sandburg had only hinted at. I had set many poems to music, had begun developing scenes, communed closely with Sandburg, and was ready.

This collaboration was to prove about one-half successful. We never did succeed in developing a story plot for that moving but plotless book. But the Sandburg *Tower of Babel* became a solid base for one of his *Twenty-Six by Corwin* and Norman's fine invention of the *Three Stuffed Shirts,* representing reaction throughout the ages, was brilliant. The vision of the *Tower* as a home for humanity, the "biggest housing project ever seen," with "Six Hour Day and Five Day Week" hit song, was mighty indeed. And instead of blaming God for shuffling all the languages and bringing disorder to the *Tower's* builders we were able to show the "Stuffed Shirts" as responsible. A fine concept. Too bad it was never finished.

We worked together, professionally again, several times, including the Roosevelt fourth-term presentation and the "Founding of the United Nations" program. One more deserves special mention. A sort of follow up to the "Ballad for Americans," a longer cantata done with words by Millard Lampell has been spoken of as my finest work. We called it originally "Abraham Lincoln Comes Home." It is the story of the funeral train that carried Lincoln's body from Washington to Springfield. It ran twenty-seven minutes, more than half the length of "Ballad." It was optioned by Warner Bros. for a film, which option kept it off the air and out of Norman's capable hands for a year. Fortunately, nobody at Warner's knew what to do with it (they were considering it for a Western presentation of some kind) and it reverted to Lampell and me.

Norman again came up with a better name for it. "A Lonesome Train." This musical legend was a profound artistic success although it was not as immediately accessible to audiences and performances as the "Ballad." Production-wise this was a deeper collaboration. Lacking a part for Paul Robeson, I worked closely with Burl Ives. A black gospel singers' group narrated and shout sang the Square Dance caller. You might say I directed with Norman, but of course his was the guiding vision that pulled it all together for the CBS broadcast in March of 1944.

It was a creative learning process to work with Norman. He is a master at finding the light, the satiric, the graceful way of handling *content.* And, like I said, I see him as a celebrator. Though his latest work, *Trivializing America* gives attention to the negative, well written as it is, I urge him to get back on the high road as soon as he decently can.

I love you, Norman.

Afterword

Norman Corwin, the writer who Studs Terkel lauds as "the bard of radio's Golden Age," has always felt strongly about important issues and has used his great gifts of language to move people's lives. The sound of his authentic voice and the power of his written words have led people, many who are now illustrious, to follow his professional examples. Writing in this collection, Charles Kuralt of CBS remembers how it began for him: "They had a book of Corwin's plays in the school library in North Carolina. I read it at 13 and knew what I wanted to try to do with my life."

For this book, we asked some of Norman's many admirers to write what they wished about radio broadcasting. Most found it difficult to resist writing about what Norman had meant to broadcasting and to them. They quickly pointed out the preeminent role that Norman played in the Golden Age of Radio from the late 1930's to the late 1940's, but noted that Norman's energies did not flag when radio became less central. He has always gone on to other victories.

The School of Journalism at the University of Southern California was very fortunate when Norman Corwin agreed to teach our students five years ago. We gained not only a man who could instruct us about radio but one who has reached the top in medium after medium—in television, cinema, magazines, and books. Norman Corwin is an example that a person with something to say and the ability to say it will find a way to say it, no matter how the face of communication changes.

Norman's students and faculty colleagues have found him to be a warm, cheerful man who celebrates life. On the occasion of his 75th birthday, we want to celebrate his life and our gratitude for his birth. We want to thank the busy contributors to this volume who have generously written great essays to honor their friend Norman, to Luther Luedtke and Jack Langguth of the School o Journalism who initiated this collection of essays, and Frances Ring who did indispensable service in soliciting and editing thi collection.

We expect this publication to mark something of a mid-point in Norman Corwin's incredibly productive career. We know that Norman's father is still going strong at 108 years of age and fully expect that for many decades to come Norman will be doing his share in all places where words count.

Bryce Nelson
Director, USC School of Journalism